Working with Time

Recognising and Using Opportunity

Suzanne Rough

authorHOUSE®

AuthorHouse™ UK Ltd.
1663 Liberty Drive
Bloomington, IN 47403 USA
www.authorhouse.co.uk
Phone: 0800.197.4150

Published by AuthorHouse   05/29/2014

ISBN: 978-1-4969-8041-0 (sc)
ISBN: 978-1-4969-8042-7 (e)

Library of Congress Control Number: 2014908778

Other Astrological Works by Suzanne Rough

Understanding the Natal Chart: An Esoteric Approach to Learning Horoscopy

Understanding Relationship: Synastry and Compository

Transitional Astrology: Giving an Esoteric Role to Orthodox Astrology

Contents

For my clients of the past three decades who brought the ideas to life.

Preface

For a student astrologer, learning the art of prediction is a good discipline because it tests the understanding of energy principles, how they express themselves, and how the different principles interact. However, prediction has no real place in Western astrology.

Unfortunately, it is all too easy to impress with a few accurate predictions. Those who visit astrologers think they want to know what is going to happen, but they do not, not really, not Westerners brought up on the idea of free will. We are confused and disempowered by predeterminism.

We would rather know about the kind of situations that are going to present themselves so that we can make conscious decisions about how to engage with them. Keeping the focus upon the circumstances, not the probable outcomes, creates opportunities for intelligent choice. This serves Western consciousness better.

This book first came into being as a teaching manual after two decades of client work during which I used to good effect, apparently, a small number of time-working techniques to help my clients identify and prepare themselves for their opportunities.

I have made some revisions for the purposes of this edition, removing case histories and observations. While they have a place in a teacher-student communication, they are not appropriate for a mass-market book.

Suzanne Rough
April 2014

Introduction

Time scales

The competent astrologer is a juggler. We juggle to blend influences, and we juggle signs and houses, planets with other planets, and planets and aspects. We juggle with different time frames and alternative time scales.

Human time is created by the human brain. It is a product of the personality in incarnation. As a basic point of reference, it uses the relationship between the sun (Endnote 1) and our planet, Earth.

The rotation of Earth upon its axis gives us our day; the movement of Earth along the ecliptic gives us our months; and a complete revolution gives us our year. This is as true for an astrologer as it is for the astronomer and for those who simply keep an eye on the time to manage their lives, even if astrologers do start their year at the spring equinox and not the first day of January.

Astrologers, however, have other time frames that use a different scale, although they express the relationship between the Sun and the Earth

It is a long-established tradition in practical astrology to make one day in the ephemeris equal to one year of human life.

There is in existence a video of Robert Hand being sworn in as the president of the American Astrological Association. One would have to go a very long way to find a more competent astrologer than Robert Hand. Hand claims to have worked with every surviving astrological tradition and has written some first-rate books. Though when it comes to answering his own question of why, in time-dynamic astrology, a day should equal a year, he sidesteps the issue entirely and says, rather disarmingly, that he simply does not know why it works, but it does.

It is highly unlikely that Hand is unaware, although one wonders why he did not want to give an uncomplicated explanation. It involves just one word: correspondence. It is the same principle expressing itself on a different level. In the course of both the year and the day, Earth moves through all twelve signs of the zodiac. It takes Earth twelve months to move through each of the signs and just twenty-four hours for it to make a complete revolution on its axis, taking in each of the signs as it turns. According to esoteric thinking, this makes the day the lower correspondence of the year.

In this short course dedicated to working with time, we will be looking at the following:

- primary directions (scale: day for a year)
- secondary directions (scale: day for a year and two hours equal one month [the lunar equivalent])
- transits (scale: real time)

There are other time-working techniques, but these are the ones that we are selecting as being most useful for identifying opportunity without getting involved in a level of detail that lures one close to the rocks of predeterminism.

Energy combinations that produce events are predetermined; the forms with which they clothe themselves are not.

Predeterminism, fate, and opportunity

The natal chart is a diagram of the celestial relationships in force at the moment that a child's independent life begins. Contained within that energy pattern is our path, which will disclose itself in time. Unless premature demise is a factor, that path will take the child into adulthood, from adulthood into old age, and then on to the doorway out of incarnation.

We spin our own paths from our psyches just as a spider spins thread from within its own body. To work with time in astrology is to pull out and put into a frame that part of his or her path that an individual will be covering at a given age, i.e., after a certain number of revolutions of Earth around the sun. Because the planets orbit at predictable speeds, it is possible to identify their mutual relations at any point in the future, as well as their relations to their positions in the birth chart. These predetermined relationships are the basis of prediction.

A person can be blown along his path as the wind blows a fallen leaf, in and out of the events and situations that will cause both pleasure and pain. Alternatively, he can move along it purposefully, recognising that the people, situations, and events he encounters are all externalising aspects of his own psyche, in a process that can help him gain an understanding and mastery of himself, and learn to act more efficiently and effectively.

Fate is created by the triad of life and time, personality pattern (see Endnote 2), and a passive consciousness. Fate exists where a man cannot resist what, in conformity with his pattern, is brought by the passage of life and time, be that pleasure or pain. In a culture that is fatalistic, the concepts that arouse an individual to change that pattern will not exist in any accessible form.

Opportunity is created by the triad of life and time, personality pattern, and an active consciousness. Opportunity is made. Regardless of whether the frame of reference is worldly success or spiritual development, the recognition of opportunity requires a perception of a relationship between life and an interactive personality. Otherwise, there will simply be times of good fortune or misfortune.

This perception of the interactive relationship between life and personality is what the West has brought to the study of astrology.

Although our understanding of free will is often confused and our attitude to fate ambivalent and inconsistent, we have admitted into consciousness the idea that fate can be challenged. The principal strategies are self-knowledge, determination, self-discipline, and, of course, an awareness of how things could be different.

Once the natal chart is drawn up, the energy pattern in force at any age in an individual's life may be ascertained using time-working techniques. Let us consider what this means.

If we were to look ahead to a newborn baby's twenty-first birthday year and saw that the planet Uranus and the tenth house were particularly active in the pattern, we would assume that independence issues would be to the fore at this age.

Using the three techniques that we are covering in this course, the pattern could be made to disclose the kind of situations and the kind of relationships from which he needed to become more independent. It would be part of the astrologer's task to explain why he should need this greater freedom and what he could do with it.

The Western astrologer would not expect to supply detailed descriptions of the personalities involved in his struggles because this would not add anything to the understanding of the principles involved. And indeed, using the three techniques that we are recommending, it would be difficult for the astrologer to supply too much detail about the form.

The Hindu astrologer, by contrast, engaged in the same task of looking ahead to the twenty-first birthday year, could be expected to focus on the personalities involved, identifying and describing, by means of the formidable analytical methods of his tradition (which rely heavily upon dispositors), the father or the employer, probably providing physical descriptions, and thereby encasing the authority principle in a specific form.

Consider the difference between a statement to the effect that, at age twenty-one, the child would be highly concerned with the issue of independence and personal freedom and that the statement that at twenty-one the child would be battling with the father or employer who is trying to hold him back.

The first is open, while the second is shut. The one recognises a developmental opportunity, while the other foretells of strife and difficulty. The one serves development and decision-making, while the other removes choice. They encompass the differences between Western and Eastern astrology. The one is anticipating opportunity, and it is the astrology of possibility; the other is fatalism and is the astrology of probability.

By now, the more philosophically minded may be asking whether there is an objective situation here. If the Western astrologer used the analytical techniques of the Hindus, would he not arrive at the same conclusion? In some instances, he might; in others, he might not. The rules of analysis that have been created by the Hindus are for use within the Hindu culture. Western culture supports different expectations, choices, and consequences. The energy principles identified would be the same, though.

In any event, if the astrologer is wise and understands esoteric law, he will refrain from giving voice to too much detail because sound fixes pattern.

It better suits Western developmental purposes to hold back on detail about form to help to keep the subject's options open longer and to encourage creative decision—making. The movement of the heavens should supply pointers to possibilities, not probabilities. The astrologer should not seek to pre-empt choice or mould the energy by anticipating outcomes in words or even in thought.

The three time-working techniques that we recommend in this course will not make an astrologer unduly influential.

Endnote

1. Traditionally, the physical sun takes the lower case; the astrologer's symbol the upper case. In practice, in a work of this kind, switching between the two can become complicated. From hereon, therefore, both Sun and Moon will take the upper case.
2. Although we are concerned here with the personality of a human being, the groupings to which humans belong (businesses, organisations, nations, cultures, etc.) have their personality aspect, too.

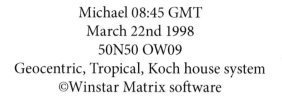

Michael 08:45 GMT
March 22nd 1998
50N50 0W09
Geocentric, Tropical, Koch house system
©Winstar Matrix software

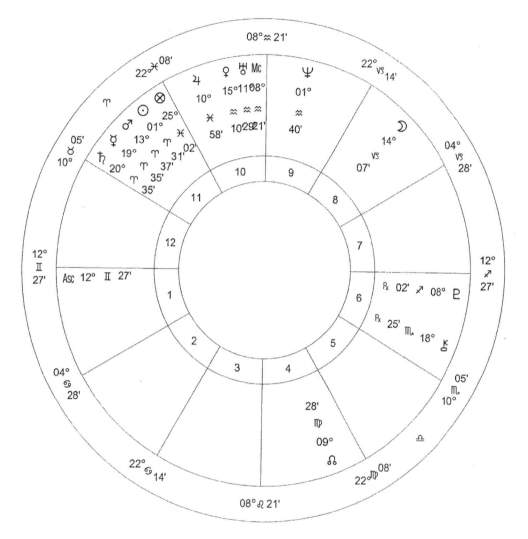

Part One

Primary Directions and
Secondary Progressions

Chapter 1

Primary Directions

As is the case with all time-working techniques, this procedure is meaningless without a natal chart. All calculations used in this lesson are based upon the birth data of Michael, born on 22 March 1998, at 08:45 in Brighton, England. We are interested in developments that will be occurring in and around his twenty-first birthday year.

Definition:
Primary directions are thusly called because they involve the Sun (the prime source) and the aspects the Sun makes as it directs itself at the other planets and the hyleg points (ascendant and descendant; midheaven (MC) and its opposite point (IC)).

Time scale:
A day for a year.

Purpose:
To identify the most basic energies in force in any given period. This is the first (prime) level of influence.

Method:
1. In the ephemeris, taking a day for a year, add as many days to the birthdate as are required to arrive at the required age. At this level, it is advisable to include in the time frame two years before the required age and four years afterward, giving a period of seven years in total.

Create a table accordingly:

age in years	☿	♀	♂	♃	♄	♅	♆	♇

2. Label the table Natal (or Radical) Sun to Progressed Planets, and make a note of the sign and degree of the natal Sun. The conventional abbreviations of radical and progressed are r and p, respectively.

3. Look at the progressing placements for each planet in the period under review to ascertain whether any planet makes an aspect to the natal Sun. The movement of the progressing Moon is not taken into account in primary directions, but is of definitive importance in the technique known as secondary directions.

4. Insert the finding in the table. No orbs of influence are allowed in this procedure. Only exact aspects are to be considered, but it is common sense to note any aspects that form just outside the period under review.

The above five points represent stage one of a five-stage procedure.

We will now go through stage one using Michael's chart. Michael's Sun is at ♈1.

1. Michael's twenty-first birthday year corresponds to 12 April 1998. This means that the seven-year review period runs from 10 April to 16 April, inclusively.

2 and 3. The table should be drawn up as:

Stage one: Natal (or radical) Sun / Progressed planets

☉ ♈1° / planets p

age in years	☿	♀	♂	♃	♄	♅	♆	♇
19								
20								
21								
22								
23			∨					
24			∨					
25								

4. There is just one aspect formed to Michael's Sun: a semi-sextile from Mars at ♉1° on 14 and 15 April.

5. **The semi-sextile sign ⚹ should be inserted in the column headed ♂ and against ages twenty-three and twenty-four.**

Comments:
- To find just one aspect in a seven-year period is not uncommon. Sometimes, there will be two or three or none at all.
- The semi-sextile may be a minor aspect, but at this level, all aspects are influential.

Interpretation:
- At ages twenty-three and twenty-four, Michael's identity will be given a greater definition by Martian energy. Mars is the ruler of the sixth house and the ruler of the sign intercepted in the eleventh houses, and it might be expected that situations involving work, health, colleagues, and friends will be agents in this process.
- As the aspect involved is a semi-sextile, the process might be expected to increase the energy around the situations, but not uncomfortably so. An increase in self-confidence is to be expected as a result of the process.

Moving on to the other stages.

Stage two: Progressed Sun and planets to natal (or radical) Moon. This involves the same procedure as stage one, but uses the placement of the natal Moon. The Sun, of course, should be included in the list of progressing planets.

Stage three: Progressed Sun and planets to natal (or radical) ascendant.
This involves the same procedure, but uses the sign and degree of the radical ascendant.

Stage four: Progressed Sun and planets to natal (or radical) MC.
This involves the same procedure, but uses the sign and degree of the radical MC.

Stage five: Progressed Sun to natal (or radical) planets.
This involves the progressing Sun and the natal placements of the planets.

Comments:
By means of these five stages, the aspects received by the radical Sun from the progressing planets, the aspects thrown by the progressing Sun to the radical positions of the planets, as well as the aspects thrown by the progressing Sun and progressing planets to the radical Moon, give a comprehensive picture of the primary influences that will be at work during the seven-year period under review. These influences will be the bedrock of the period.

At first glance, this may seem a long and complicated process, but it takes very little time at all, especially if table templates are drafted in advance.

Let us look at stages two to five using Michael's chart.

Stage two: Progressed Sun and planets to natal (or radical) Moon

☽ ♑ 14° / ☉p & planets p

age in years	☉	☿	♀	♂	♃	♄	♅	♆	♇
19									
20									
21									
22									
23									
24									
25									

Findings: There are no aspects in the period under review, but on 9 April, the day that corresponds to Michael's eighteenth birthday year, there was an important aspect: ☿R□☽ that will produce emotional tension. The Moon represents the emotional identity, as well as the past and the mother, and in Michael's chart, it is in the eighth house, the house of emotional regeneration. In his chart, Mercury is to be found in the eleventh house, indicating that friendship and acceptance by others may be instrumental in this emotionally tense situation. As Mercury rules the fifth house, the house of creativity and individuality, as well as the ascendant, these tensions involving acceptance by others may dent his self-image, and he is likely to bring the memory of it through into the period under review. At the primary level, aspects to the natal Moon are always impactful.

Stage three: Progressed Sun and planets to natal (or radical) ascendant

Aˢᶜ♊12° / ☉p & planets p

age in years	☉	☿	♀	♂	♃	♄	♅	♆	♇
19									
20									
21		✳R							
22									
23									
24									
25									

Findings: When Michael is twenty-one, retrograde Mercury will make a sextile aspect to his radical ascendant. This means, of course, that at the same time, it will be trining the descendant or the cusp of the seventh house. As noted above, radical Mercury is in the eleventh house of Michael's chart, and this indicates that there are positive developments regarding friendship and acceptance by others that have a markedly feel-good factor. The trine to the cusp of the seventh indicates that there are new friendships or a friendship of importance

6

forming at this time. Maybe a friend becomes a partner. The sextile aspect to the ascendant indicates an opportunity to restore the confidence after the knocks at eighteen years.

Stage four: Progressed Sun and planets to natal (or radical) MC

MC♈︎ 8° / ☉p & planets p

age in years	☉	☿	♀	♂	♃	♄	♅	♆	♇
19									
20									
21									
22									
23			⋁						
24									
25									

Findings: When Michael is twenty-three, a progressing Venus makes a semi-sextile aspect to the MC. This indicates positive developments in career and lifestyle at this age. With Venus being in the tenth house natally and the ruler of the fifth and twelfth houses, this indicates that, albeit in a subtle way, Michael is able to incorporate more of what he values into his career and lifestyle.

Stage five: Progressed Sun to natal (or radical) planets

☉p / **Planets r**

age in years	☿♈︎19°	♀♒︎15°	♂♈︎13°	♃♓︎11°	♄♈︎20°	♅♒︎11°	♆♒︎1°	♇♐︎8°
19					☌			
20								
21								
22								
23								
24								
25								

Findings: Although there is only one aspect formed by the progressing Sun in the period under review, it is an important one: ☉p ☌ ♄. At the primary level, aspects involving Saturn are very decisive and indicate a year of much heaviness, frustration, and restriction. Saturn natally is in the eleventh house, and this indicates that the heart of the problem appears to be friendship and acceptance. This theme has appeared before in the form of ☿R□☽r, experienced just before the period under review commenced, at age eighteen.

It may be seen in the ephemeris that also at age eighteen, the progressed Sun conjuncts natal Mercury in the eleventh house, which reinforces the friendship/acceptance theme, and adds that of communication.

Reviewing the five stages as applied to Michael's chart.

- The total amount of primary aspects picked up across the five stages is not great, but there is a marked trend in evidence: as the twenties advance, there is an increase in positive aspects and opportunities positively experienced.

- This is in marked contrast to the trying experiences that close the teens. We can conclude from this that Michael's late teens will be a challenging time, which is revealing because his circumstances at this time will be externalising the Saturnian mindset in a very obvious way. As Saturn natally is in the eleventh house, this may be expected to feature problems with integrating with others, which will be a recurring theme in his life.

It is the responsibility of the astrologer concerned with spiritual development to present every experience, positive or negative, from the point of view of the personality as an opportunity, and to be able to offer, through the identification of the principles involved, not only insights into what is to be learned or experienced, but the reasons why they should be didactic. These explanations should not be bland clichés about struggle being character-building, but have specific reference to the theme of the lifetime. To do this, the astrologer must have fully examined and understood the natal chart.

Astrology students are advised to repeat this exercise to analyse an eventful period of their own lives to get a feel for the way contacts at the primary level manifest.

Chapter 2

Secondary Directions

As is the case with all time-working techniques, this procedure is meaningless without a natal chart. All calculations used in this lesson are based upon the birth data of Michael, who was born on 22 March 1998, at 08:45 in Brighton, England. We are interested in developments that will be occurring in and around his twenty-first birthday year.

Definition:
Secondary directions are concerned with the formative effect of the lunar influence (the secondary source) upon the planets and hylegs that receive it.

This technique, which gives a relatively detailed picture of a one-year period, is best used in conjunction with primary directions to create a context for the energies at work before, during, and after this period.

Time scale:
  i) A day for a year
  ii) Two hours worth of lunar motion for one month

Purpose:
  • Indicates the stage reached in the Sun-Moon cycle (see Endnote 1).
  • Identifies the way in which the available energies will manifest themselves in everyday life. The house position of the progressing Moon is of paramount importance here.

Method:
If using computer software, create a chart for the time of birth, but use the date that corresponds to the birthday year. This document is the secondary chart. Then, with this document, proceed as directed from step six below.

  1. In the ephemeris, taking a day for a year, add as many days to the birthdate as are required to arrive at the required age.

2. Note the sidereal equivalent of midnight (or noontime, depending upon the ephemeris) on this day.

3. From this figure, deduct the sidereal time at midnight (or noon) on the day of birth.

4. To this result, add the local sidereal time of birth, according to which the natal chart was constructed. This gives what is called the progressed MC.

5. Construct another chart, as if constructing a natal chart, but using the progressed MC, and place all planets (for the time of birth on the day that corresponds to the birthday year under review) except the Moon in the figure. The Moon needs special treatment because it requires twelve placements: one for each month of the year under review.

6. Calculate the Moon's motion on the day that corresponds to the birthday year (this will be its placement on the day following the year under review minus its placement on the day that represents the present birthday year), and divide it by twelve. This gives its motion in two hours, which, using this time scale, is the equivalent of one month.

7. Create a column using the Moon's position at the time of birth of the birthday equivalent. This gives its placement for the first month after the birthday. Then add, progressively, the two-hourly increments to find a placement for every month thereafter. The Moon's average two-hourly motion will be slightly in excess of one degree, but as its rate of movement fluctuates so much, it is desirable to calculate it.

8. Insert the Moon's twelve monthly placements in the chart, thus:

$$☽ ————— ☽$$

9. Calculate the aspects cast each month by the progressing Moon to planets and hylegs in both the progressed and natal charts.

10. Note the findings in a systematic manner.

11. Interpret the findings.

Comments:

1. With its eleven stages, this process is more labour-intensive than the previous exercise, but it is a very rewarding undertaking (see Endnote 2). This is the level that is likely to reveal the circumstances that have motivated a client to contact the astrologer.

2. This pattern holds for a year, and the planets' relationships to each other should be noted, but use only tight orbs: zero to one degree. Note also if any planet changes house.

3. Among astrologers, there is not a consensus on the matter of whether the progressed chart should be constructed using the house cusps for the place of residence at the age attained or whether the progressed chart should continue to use the place of birth, even though the subject may have moved. Students are encouraged to try both options using their own charts and those of people known to them to arrive at their own conclusions.

We will now do this exercise using Michael's chart, using the secondary level to add to what we know already about this time of his life. Although the primary directions (see previous lesson) reveal nothing of significance for that year specifically, we have an overview of developments in the seven-year period that spans his nineteenth to twenty-sixth years.

Stage one: Counting on from the day of birth in the ephemeris, we remind ourselves that 12 April 1998 corresponds to Michael's twenty-first birthday year.

Stage two: Find sidereal time at midnight on **12 April**	13 hrs	20 mins
Stage three: Deduct sidereal time at midnight on **22 March** (day of birth)	11 hrs	57 mins
Result	**1 hr**	**23 ruins**
Stage four: Add local sidereal time of birth (taken from natal chart)	20 hrs	43 mins
Result	**22 hrs**	**06 ruins**

Stage five: Find house cusps for 50° N 50' / 0° W when the MC is 22 hrs 06 mins 09' and construct a chart.

Stage six: Calculate the Moon's daily motion on 12 April and from the ephemeris.

Position of Moon   1) at Midnight on 13th = ♏ $4° 30'$

2) at Midnight on 12th = ♎ $22° 37'$
daily motion = $11° \underline{53'}$

Stage 7: Find monthly motion if daily motion is the equivalent of 1 year:

$$\frac{11^{\circ}\,53'}{12} = \frac{713'}{12} = 59.4' = 59'$$

Month, from 22nd	longitude	add	result	rounded up *
March	♎ 26° 57'	59'	♎ 27° 56'	♎ 28°
April	♎ 27° 56'	59'	♎ 28° 55'	♎ 29°
May	♎ 28° 55'	59'	♎ 29° 54'	♏ 0°
June	♎ 29° 54'	59'	♏ 0° 53'	♏ 1°
July	♏ 0° 53'	59'	♏ 1° 52'	♏ 2°
August	♏ 1° 52'	59'	♏ 2° 51'	♏ 3°
September	♏ 2° 51'	59'	♏ 3° 50'	♏ 4°
October	♏ 3° 50'	59'	♏ 4° 49'	♏ 5°
November	♏ 4° 49'	59'	♏ 5° 48'	♏ 6°
December	♏ 5° 48'	59'	♏ 27° 47'	♏ 7°
January	♏ 6° 47'	59'	♏ 7° 46'	♏ 8°
February	♏ 7° 46'			

Stage 8: Insert into figure, thus:

☽ ♏ 26° 57'----------☽ ♏ 7° 46'

or

☽ ♏ 27°--------☽ ♏ 8°

* Rounding up may be done at this stage, unless strict accuracy is required.

Stages nine and ten: Calculate aspects for each month and note findings in a systematic fashion.

Month, from 22nd	aspects to natal placements	aspects to progressed placements
March ♎ 27°	-	-
April ♎ 28°	-	-
May ♎ 29°	-	☍ ♂ △ M
June ♏ 0°	-	-
July ♏ 1°	⚺ ☉ □ ♆	-

August ♏ 2°		-	□♇
September ♏ 3°		-	△♇
October ♏ 4°		-	-
November ♏ 5°		-	-
December ♏ 6°		-	-
January ♏ 7°		-	⊻♀
February ♏ 8°		□♇ ⊻♀	-

Interpreting the findings

If students experience difficulty at first in interpreting secondary aspect, the problem, almost invariably, arises because they find it hard to shift in their thinking about the role of the Moon from being the symbol of the past in natal chart interpretation to being the vitaliser in progressed charts. To understand the connection between the two, though, is to understand a great deal about the nature of our personal realities. The developments brought about in our lives that we capture at the secondary level are the product of our conditioned minds, and our minds have been conditioned by the past.

Michael: Secondary chart for 21st birthday year
(April 21 1998 / 08:45 GMT / 50N50 0W09)

Geocentric, Tropical, Koch house system

©Winstar Matrix software

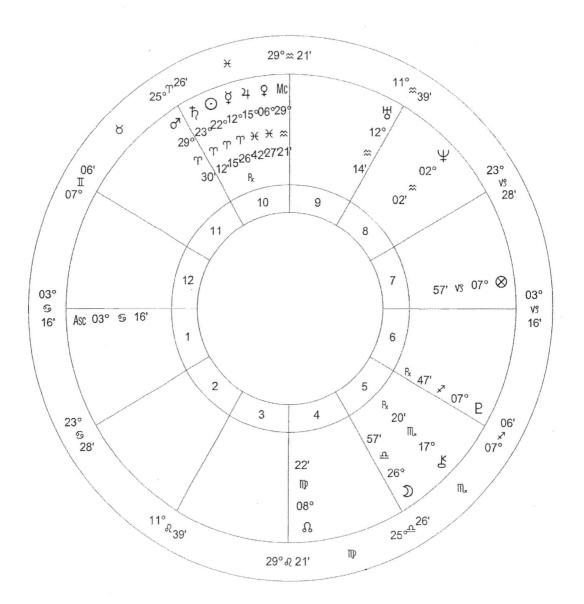

The secondary chart: Considerations

1. Ascertain the relationship between the progressed Sun and the progressed Moon. How far away from the Sun is the Moon?

2. The house in which the Moon is found in the progressed chart indicates that this area of life will be an area of particular concern. For the duration of the time that the Moon occupies this house, this area of life will be the assemblage point for events and experiences. Also to be considered is the house that the Moon with its twelve positions would occupy if it were to be inserted into the framework of the natal chart. This area of life acts as an important subinfluence (see Endnote 3).

3. When the Moon reaches the final five degrees of a progressed house, there will be a development of considerable significance that will bring to a conclusion the experiences undergone while the Moon has been in that house. From this point onward, the influence of the next house becomes very apparent.

4. When it makes an aspect to any planet or hyleg, the Moon activates that principle. If the aspect is stressful, that principle will be activated in a challenging way and will behave in a way that is perceived to be disruptive in the house in which that planet is found by progression and in the house that the planet is found natally.

5. The houses of which the activated planet is the ruler, both natally and by progression, must also be considered. If the aspect is harmonious, the Moon activates that principle in a harmonious way, and it will express itself in a way that is perceived to be productive and constructive in the house that the planet is found by progression and in the house that the planet is found natally.

The reverse is the case if the contact is stressful.

6. The aspects made by the Moon to natal and progressed planets are of equal weight.

Stage twelve: Integrating the primary and secondary levels

Let us apply these considerations to Michael's charts.

1. Michael's progressed Sun is in Aries and has moved from the eleventh into the tenth house, and his progressed Moon is in Libra in the fifth house. The aspect between them is a separating opposition aspect. This indicates that in the birthday previous year, when the opposition aspect was exactly on twenty-one degrees, the tension in Michael's mind between his conditioning and his true identity had reached a critical stage. The conflict would have involved his awareness of himself as an individual (fifth house) and of his true identity as a group person.
   - As the progressing Sun has moved into the tenth house, it is to be expected that Michael's career is an agent in process of creating within him awareness of this conflict between individuality and loyalty and responsibility to the group or team.

- Against the natal house frame, Michael's progressing Sun is still in the eleventh house. It is to be expected that in his twenty-first birthday year, this tension will be dispersing as a result of his having found a way to better synthesise the two.

2. In the progressed chart, Michael's Moon is found in the fifth house; in the natal chart, it is also in the fifth house, but moving toward the closing degrees of that house. This indicates that creativity is Michael's basic concern at this time. When the Moon is in the fifth house, a person is inclined to be experimental and frequently takes up new creative activities. Not all of these activities may prove suitable, but it is very commonly the case that one may prove to be of particular interest. When the Moon moves into the sixth house, this new creative activity frequently begins to change the way a person thinks about making his contribution through work. Often, he will want this new activity to be incorporated into his work.
3. Michael's progressing Moon is near the beginning of the fifth house, indicating that his period experimentation with creativity and possibly sex is just beginning.
4. In the May of his twenty-first birthday year, the progressing Moon makes:
   - an opposition aspect to progressed Mars in the eleventh house (Mars rules the sixth and eleventh house natally and the fifth and eleventh house by progression)
   - a trine to the progressed MC

This indicates that developments at work that appear to favour Michael's career may have to be achieved at the expense of leaving behind friends and colleagues or entering into overt competition with them.

5. In the July of that birthday year, the progressing Moon:

   - Enters the sign Scorpio and makes a quincunx aspect with the Sun (ruling the fourth house natally and the third house by progression).
   - Makes a square to Neptune (in the ninth house natally and the ruler of the eleventh house, in the eighth house by progression and the ruler of the tenth house).

This indicates that the tension between career and comradeship persists and appears to have implications for Michael's domestic arrangements. A severance in a friendship may occur. He appears to be emotionally upset by this. Remember his conditioned mind's default setting (see Endnote 1). This situation persists into August.

6. In the September of that year, the progressing Moon makes a trine to the progressed ascendant (and, by virtue of this, a sextile to the descendant). This indicates that personally, things are improving, particularly in respect of close relationships.
7. In the January of that birthday year, the Moon makes a semi-sextile to progressed Pluto (in the sixth house and ruler of the sixth house natally and the fifth house by progression).
8. In the following month, the progressed Moon makes a square to the natal MC. This indicates that as his twenty-first birthday year draws to a close, Michael is having

serious doubts about his choice of career and is wondering whether he should not try and use his creative energy differently. Poor health may drive home this message. As this birthday year closes, Michael's progressing Moon still has a long way to go through the fifth house. This will mean that on the matter of his search for a new creative frame, he has some way to go yet.

9. This is the time to look back at the primary directions and see if they offer any clues as the outcome of this situation. The aspects that form in the period under review form between ages twenty-two and twenty-four. They include a semi-sextile between Mars and the Sun and a semi-sextile between Venus and the MC. We have to conclude, therefore, that it may not be until he is approaching his midtwenties that Michael is able to move on in any meaningful way from this situation involving the use of his creative energy and his career.

Students are advised to repeat this exercise for a memorable year of their own lives in order to get a feel for the way that contact at the secondary level manifest in everyday life.

Endnotes

1.   The Sun-Moon Cycle, seen through the Secondary Chart.

From the moment of birth, captured in the natal chart, the heavens are moving. This movement is scaled down by reducing a year to a day, but it continues nevertheless. The rapidly moving, progressing Moon changes its relation to the progressing Sun, and the rate of motion of which is significantly slower.

A Sun-Moon cycle takes around twenty-eight years to complete. There are three different ways of measuring it:

1. The return of the progressing Moon to its natal placement and therefore to the relationship that the Moon had to the Sun at birth. The separation of the conjunction aspect between the progressing and natal Moon sees a new cycle commence.
2. The arrival of the progressing Moon to the place of the natal Sun (or progressing Sun). This is called the synodic cycle. Again, the separation of the conjunction aspect between these two luminaries sees a new cycle commence.
3. The arrival of the progressing Moon to the ascendant, which means that the passage of the Moon through the twelfth house closes the cycle and that the movement of the Moon across the ascendant commences a new cycle. The position of the Moon at birth will determine the age at which the first cycle, which is usually a partial cycle, will close.

In each case, the method is the same and requires the creation of a secondary chart. What differs is the point at which the new cycle is considered to commence. Students are advised to consider all three options and decide for themselves which they prefer to use.

The theme of this cycle is the refinement of the identity that is defined by the sign and house position of the natal Sun. The changing relationship between the Sun and the Moon indicates the way in which the conditioned mind alternatively helps (harmonious aspects between the progressing Moon and Sun) and offers challenging stressful aspects between the two) to the unfolding of the true identity.

In very many cases, the progressed Sun will remain in the same house that the radical Sun is found in the natal chart, and this means that this Sun-Moon cycle is in the service of the basic developmental requirement of the lifetime. If the Sun does change houses, however, because the signs of short and long ascension are on the ascendant or the chart contains intercepted signs, the area of life represented by the new house needs to be considered as temporarily important to the unfolding of the identity.

The position of the progressing Sun against the natal house frame needs also to be considered. During the course of an average life, the progressing Sun may move through four or five houses; and these new positions will provide important subinfluences in the task of unfolding the identity.

The sign and position of the natal Moon will indicate the conditioned mind's default setting. In Michael's case, his natal Moon is in Capricorn in the eighth house and is the ruler of the second house.

This indicates that Michael responds to the memory of being closely involved with others and taking responsibility, including financial responsibility, for them. He fears disagreement leading to unpopularity and rejection.

2. Although this may seem a very time-consuming exercise, it is not, and familiarity with the process will shorten it considerably.

3. The influence upon the progressing Moon of the progressed and natal houses is the subject of a new work by the author, *Making the Journey of the Lifetime.*

Part One Appendix

Refinements to the basic technique of secondary directions

The information in this appendix is separate because it will be assimilated more quickly and more easily once the basic technique has been mastered.

1. Progressing the Ascendant and MC

This is a somewhat fiddly procedure but worth doing because aspects to the ascendant and MC are such important significators.

A purist could point out that as the hyleg points cast no rays; they can receive planetary influences only when the aspect is in conjunction, square, or opposition aspect. When working with astrology, however, it soon becomes apparent that the hyleg points are as receptive of harmonious aspects as they are of the challenging.

The method is not dissimilar from that used for primary directions, but it is much easier to capture this information once the secondary chart has been constructed for reasons that will become obvious.

1. Take the progressed MC from the progressed chart, and apply this to the table of houses for the place of birth. Advancing it by one degree for every year, and note the changing movement on the ascendant.
   * Thus in Michaels's case, the progressed MC, taken from the secondary chart, is twenty-nine degrees.
2. Advance this for some years at the rate one degree per year, and for the sake of comprehensiveness, go back one year.

Age	progressed A^c (at 50° 50' North)	progressed M
20	♋ 2° ⊼ Ψ_p	♒28
21	**♋ 3°**	**♒29° . ⚹ ♂_p**
22	♋ 4°	♓0° ⚹ ♂_p
23	♋ 5°	♓1° ⚹ ♂_p
24	♋ 6°	♓2°
25	♋ 7° ⊼ ♀_p	♓3°

Because of obliquity, the ascendant may not progress at a uniform rate of one degree per year, so it is advisable to check this out against the tables. In this case, however, the movement is quite even.

3. Check the natal planets against this data.
   - In Michael's case, the progressing hylegs receive no aspects from natal planets.

4. Repeat the exercise using the progressed planets. This is where it starts to gets fiddly because the secondary chart drafted from Michael's twenty-first year (12 April 1998) applies to only that birthday year. Use the chart check out whether there are any planets making aspects to either ♋3° or♒29° (we have checked out the progressing Moon already in stage ten), and note any findings.
   - It will be seen that there is a sextile from progressed Mars at ♈29°.

5. Then move on to the next day (13 April, which represents Michael's twenty-second birthday year) in the ephemeris and check out planetary positions on this day against the progressed hylegs for his twenty-second year, ♋ 4° and ♓0 ° Note the change of sign on the MC: It will bring about a change in the approach to the career and in the values generally.
   - Mars is still making that sextile to the MC. Note this against his twenty-second year.

6. Move on to the next day in the ephemeris. Do this through 16 April, which represents Michael's twenty-third, twenty-fourth, and twenty-fifth birthday years. Remember to look back to 11 April to find out the state of play on Michael's twentieth birthday.

7. Integrate these findings with the originals. It will be seen that they add more detail:
   - The quincunx made by Neptune to the progressed ascendant at age twenty automatically makes a semi-sextile to the descendant and indicates an idealised relationship, creating in him confusion about his own way of presenting and conducting himself in the world.
   - The sextile from Mars to the progressed MC for a period of three years from twenty-one to twenty-four indicates that much energy is being expended in support of the career.
   - The quincunx from Pluto to the ascendant (automatically making a semi-sextile to the descendant) indicates an intense relationship situation that provokes a lot of change in the way he presents and conducts himself in the world.

2. Aspects between the Planets

Again, these are not technically primary or secondary directions, but aspects between planets exert a significant influence (see Endnote l).

In the secondary chart, look to see if any progressed planet (excluding the progressed Sun and Moon) occupy the same degree as any planet in the natal chart or in the progressed chart. Use only exact aspects.

- In Michael's case, there is a semi-sextile (at fifteen degrees) between natal Venus in the tenth house and progressed Jupiter also in the tenth house natally and by progression. This contact from Jupiter indicates a more flexible approach to his career in this year. As Venus rules the fifth house in both the natal and progressed chart, this may also indicate a love affair, involving sexual experimentation and, as Venus also rules the eleventh and twelfth, a new companion(s) and a changed attitude to group activities. Look in the ephemeris to see how many days (years) Jupiter holds this contact with Venus (see Endnote 2).There is no aspect between any of the progressed planets

Endnotes

1. The extent of the significance will depend upon the planet, but aspects involving even minor aspects the outer planets will produce a marked effect upon the expression of the faster moving planet. Contact between Uranus and an inner planet could produce a year full of surprises.
2. Be aware that in the case of the outer planets, they can hold the same degree for months in real time. At the rate of one year for a day, this represents large proportion of a lifetime. This means that by progression, an outer planet can maintain contact with a natal inner planet or a hyleg for years. Such contacts mark a person's reality in a very pronounced way, either encouraging or constraining in accordance with the planet. It is the astrologer's job to be aware of when such contacts form and when finally they separate.

Part Two

Transits

Chapter 1

Transits: Overview

There will be few people seriously interested in astrology, whether clients or practitioners, who do not know what a transit is. What they understand this term to be is, properly speaking, a longitudinal transit. There are also declinational transits (see Endnote 1). Both use real time.

Longitudinal Transits

The definition of a transit given by Sepharial, the great British astrologer of the midtwentieth century, is "an ephemeral passage of a planet over the place of a significator in the horoscope, or the place to which it has progressed by direction after birth." This has a great merit in that it talks about significators, not simply planets, as a modem definition would.

- All planets are significators (or representatives) in that they rule an area of life (i.e. they rule the house that bears on its cusp the sign of zodiac of which that planet is the ruler, and all the things that fall within that house). For example, if, as in Michael's chart, the sign Cancer is on the cusp of second house, then the Moon is the significator of all things governed by the second house (money, possessions, and values). This is a matter to be ascertained from individual birth charts and the progressed charts. Every transiting planet is a significator and every transited planet, as well. This means that when two planets create a relationship, they bring together two the two areas of life they rule.
- A planet will acquire new territory as new signs come to occupy progressed house cusps. Such detail is additional to that supplied by the natal chart, and it does not replace it.
- All planets, both transiting and transited, are tenants of a house in the natal chart and may move into a different house as the chart is progressed.

Inner planets are those whose the orbits are within that of the Sun: Moon, Mercury, and Venus. Superior planets are those whose orbits are beyond those of the Sun.

Outer planets are those the orbits of which are beyond that of Saturn: Chiron, Uranus, Neptune, and Pluto.

For the purposes of this study of transits, we will group the planets somewhat differently.

To summarise: When considering the effect of transits, serious astrologers must always consider the house the transiting planet occupies in the natal and progressed chart and the house or houses it rules because all these areas of life will be involved in the expression of the transit. Transiting planets are agents for those areas of life. Similarly, the house that the transited planet rules must be considered, as well as that occupied natally and by progression.

Immediately, then, we have identified a shortcoming in the astrology cookbooks: They cannot deal with the planets as significators or tenants, because this is a matter for individual birth charts. This knocks out essential detail pertaining to the transit situation. No serious student of astrology can afford to become reliant upon such books.

Other considerations:

1. A transit to the progressed placement of a planet or hyleg is every bit as impactful as a transit to the natal placement. There is no meaningful distinction to be made.
2. Equally, a transiting planet is as effective an agent for the house or houses that it rules by progression, as it is for those that it rules natally.
3. Although there may be a truth in Sepharial's claim that "aspects of the planets have not the same influence," the distinction to be made is the same as that between a conjunction and any other aspect in natal horoscopy. Technically, a conjunction is the most powerful aspect, but it does not mean that other aspects are not powerful. The same is true of transits: The conjunction may be the most powerful, but the square and the opposition too are very powerful, and the trine and sextile are significant in their influence. We will look at this matter again: In this matter, there is a distinction to be made between inner and outer planets.
4. Where Scorpio, Aquarius, and Pisces are concerned, two rulers (i.e. Mars and Pluto, Saturn and Aquarius, Jupiter and Neptune) should be considered significators of the houses ruled by those signs.
5. When a sign is intercepted in a house, the ruler of the intercepted sign becomes a second significator of the things governed by that house, the first being the ruler of the sign on the cusp.

Observing planetary protocol

Being clear about the way the influence is flowing is fundamental to art understanding of transits.

-   As it approaches a slower planet, a faster-moving planet comes into its sphere of influence. Thus, it is that the Moon never influences but is only influenced by transiting activity and that Pluto is never influenced. Pluto can only influence.
-   A planet never alters its nature. A slower-moving planet elicits a response from the faster, but that response will be consistent with its nature. Thus, it is that each planet

has a number of different modes, one for each response elicited by a slower-moving planet. Pluto alone, as the slowest-moving planet, has only one mode.

- A planet is always a significator (i.e. an agent for the house that it governs in the progressed and natal chart), and it will feed that influence back into the area or areas of life that it governs.
- A stationary planet is very powerful. This condition enhances the power of the inner planets.

To summarise: It is an astrological law that the slower-moving planet influences the faster. This law is in no way modified in respect to transiting activity.

Planetary motion

In the table below, we give certain data about the motions of the planets. An astrologer needs to have an awareness of the relative speed of the planets because this enables him to assess the power of a transit. Transits do not occur singly, and in multiple transit situations, an astrologer needs to know which is going to be the most dominant influence.

planet	average amount of time taken to travel the $360°$ of the zodiac	average motion per calendar year (365 days) in arc degrees	average speed per calendar month (30 days) in arc degrees	average speed per day (24 hours) in arc minutes
☉	1 year	$360°$	$30°$	$60'\,(=1°)$
☽	28 days	$4{,}694°$	$391°$	$782'\,(=13°)$
☿	192 days	$686°$	$57°$	$114'\,(=1°\,54')$
♀	216 days	$610°$	$51°$	$102'\,(=1°\,42')$
♂	684 days	$194°$	$167.°$	$33'$
♃	12 years	$30°$	$2.5°$	$5'$
♄	28 years	$12.9°$	$1.07°$	$2.14'$
	50 years	$7.2°$	$0.6°$	$1.2'$
♅	84 years	$4.3°$	$0.36°$	$0.72'$
♆	168 years	$2.1°$	$0.18°$	$0.36'$
♇	312 years	$1.2°$	$0.1°$	$0.2'$

The point of knowing this data is not to locate the planet (the ephemeris exists for this), but to develop a working awareness of relative motion.

- Neptune's motion is 1.86 times greater than that of Pluto.
- Uranus' motion is 3.7 times greater than that of Pluto.
- Chiron's motion is 6.4 times greater than that of Pluto.
- Saturn's motion is 11.1 times greater than that of Pluto.
- Jupiter's motion is 26 times greater than that of Pluto.
- Mars' motion is 166.5 times greater than that of Pluto.
- The Sun's motion is 316.3 times greater than that of Pluto.

- Venus' motion is 527.2 times greater than that of Pluto.
- Mercury's motion is 593.1 times greater than that of Pluto.
- The Moon's motion is 4,067 times greater than that of Pluto.

Faced with this data, one is left in no doubt of why the transits of Pluto are so powerful.

Inner planets are those whose orbits are within that of the Sun: the Moon, Mercury, and Venus. Superior planets are those whose orbits of which are beyond those of the Sun.

Outer planets are those the orbits of which are beyond that of Saturn: Chiron, Uranus, Neptune, and Pluto.

For the purposes of our study of transits, we will be grouping the planets somewhat differently (see Chapter 2)

Retrogradation

All the planets go retrograde at some point in the calendar year, and some do so more than once. Retrogradation is a phenomenon of which the astrologer must be aware, both in terms of understanding the prolonging effect this stands to have on certain transits and also in terms of the effect that retrogradation has upon a person's experience of a transit. We will look at his matter in the next lesson.

The enhanced strength given to inner planets when they go stationary in preparation for going retrograde or back to direct has already been noted.

In this lesson, we are focusing upon the time aspect, emphasising how important it is for an astrologer to check out a transiting planet's progress with the ephemeris to ascertain whether, having cleared a significator, it might return to it by retrograde motion.

Aspects

When a transiting planet makes an aspect to a significator, regardless of whether it is an inner or outer planet, the contact is of the same nature as that made by two planets in a similar aspectual relationship in a natal chart (squares, quincunxes, and oppositions are a stressful blending; sextiles and trines are harmonious). Only these major aspects need to be considered.

In the matter of the aspects and their relative strength, however, there is a distinction to be made between the inner planets, the superior planets, and the outer planets.

- In the case of the inner planets, Sepharial's claim that the conjunction aspect is the most powerful is borne out. Transits from all other angles, whether stressful or harmonious, are comparatively slight in their effects. To this pattern, transiting Jupiter, although a superior planet, conforms.

- In the case of Saturn, the other superior planet, the conjunction is the most impactful, but squares and oppositions from Saturn are also marked in their effect. Harmonious aspects from Saturn are less so.
- In the case of the outer planets, the conjunction, square, and opposition are all of their impact.
- In all cases, the harmonious aspects indicate cooperation between the planets involved, and the stressful aspects indicate a challenging relationship.
- The conjunction is variable depending upon the planets concerned and upon a person's ability to handle such an intense energy: What may be experienced positively by one person may be negative to another.
- Whether made by inner or outer planets, conjunctions indicate a state of affairs arising in person's consciousness, whereas squares and oppositions indicate a state of affairs that challenges a person from the outside. Similarly, the sextile indicates a self-generated sense of well-being, whereas the trine indicates that the agency of another is likely to be involved.

The Lunar Nodes

The lunar nodes move around the ecliptic in retrograde motion, taking approximately nineteen years to cover the 360 degrees. Transits of planets to the natal lunar nodes are of importance as are transits of the lunar nodes to natal placements. The nodes, like the Moon as a body, absorb the influence from the transiting planet.

Orbs of Influence

In this matter, there is a marked lack of consensus among astrologers, and we must acknowledge that the situation is likely to be influenced by the degree of sensitivity that a person has.

Somewhat more cynically, we must also acknowledge that the degree of practical experience that an astrologer has is also likely to influence this matter. An astrologer with a lot of practical experience is likely to use narrower orbs than a theorist.

The following recommendations should be used only as guidelines.

planet	orbs approaching, all aspects	orbs retreating, all aspects
☽ ☊ ☋	depends upon the planet they are transiting / will take the orb of the transited planet	depends upon the planet they are transiting / will take the orb of the transited planet
☿ ♀	exact only / but if transiting a slower-moving planet they will take the orb of influence of that planet	no
☉ ♃	1° / if transiting a slower-moving planet, they will take the orb of influence of that planet	no
♂	2° / at its most powerful 1° / if transiting a slower-moving planet it will take orb of influence of that planet but will always be at its most powerful 1° from exact	no
♄	3° / but if transiting a slower-moving planet it will take the orb of influence of that planet	2° · still very influential 1° after exact
⚷ ♅ ♆	3° / but if transiting a slower-moving planet they will take the orb of influence of that planet	1°
♇	5°	2°

In this matter, it should be noted that Mars, in conformity with its impulsive nature, acts in advance of itself, as it were, whereas Saturn retains its grip.

The Effects of Precession

The first point of Aries (the point of interception of the ecliptic and the equator) is precessing at an average rate of 50.25 arc seconds per year along the equator. This means that every year, it takes transiting planets a little longer to reach the given point in the zodiac because they have moved backward just slightly. Over a lifetime of, say eighty years, this little bit amounts to a substantial 1°7'.

Logically, therefore in Michael's eightieth year his Sun which is at ♈1°31' in his natal chart will be transited exactly only when another planet reaches ♈2° 38' in his natal chart

How important is the matter of precession to the practising astrologer?

Essentially, it depends upon the kind of work that he is doing. If it is event-oriented, then he needs to be aware of precession and prepared to add a precessional increment to each of his natal planets every year. In practice, a transit is likely to trigger an event when it is aligned with the natal placement and another when it is aligned with the natal placement plus the increment. But anyone working with event-oriented astrology should be prepared to do his own research into this matter.

Please note that precession increments are never added to progressed placements that use a different time system.

For the astrologer concerned with the development of consciousness, then this is a less pressing matter because it is the whole process and not simply the events brought by a process that is his concern. It is important that a practising astrologer has awareness of precession because it will explain why in the chart of the older client, a process does not end at the time the ephemeris gives as the time that a transiting planet separates from the transited. If that transiting planet goes stationary or goes back by retrograde motion into the arc space of the precessional increment, this could extend a process for many months.

An astrologer of this kind needs to have a precessional perspective, and although it is not necessary for him to calculate the increment every year, he should know at least what precession amounts to in every decade of a person's life.

This we give below.

age in years	precessional increment in arc minutes and seconds
10	8'22"
20	16'45"
30	25' 8"
40	33'31"
50	41'53"
60	50'16"
70	58'39"
80	10 7'

As a conclusion to this overview, let us pull together the points that have been made and check them out against an example: the transits that will be in force on Michael's twenty-first birthday and the year that follows.

In this exercise, we are focusing on the technique itself. We will deal with interpretation in the next lesson when we will assess what kind of day Michael can expect on his twenty-first birthday, having placed that day in a context.

Example

To examine the transits in force on Michael's twenty-first birthday and the year that follows, we need the following:

- Michael's natal chart prepared for 22 March 1998, 08:45, Brighton, England
- a progressed chart prepared for his twenty-first birthday year using the day for a year method
- as Michael's twenty-first birthday falls on 22 March 2019, an ephemeris showing planetary positions for that year

1. Distinguish the transits that will be in force only on Michael's birthday from those that will be in force during the twelve months that follow.
    - The speed at which the inner planets and the Sun move means that, if they make contact with significators on his birthday, they will soon move on. Their influence will be only for that day unless they make a station. They represent Category 1 transits.
    - Mars and Jupiter take rather longer to clear a given point and have orbs of influence when they are advancing. They need to be considered separately as Category 2 transits.
    - Saturn and the outer planets have significant orbs of influence when they are advancing and may take a very long time to clear a given point. They represent Category 3 transits.
    - The transiting nodes represent Category 4 transits.

2. Consider the effect of precession.

At twenty-one years, the precessional increment is *50.25* arc sees x 21 = 17' 35.6"= **18'.**

To get a feel for what precession means, add to Michael's natal placements:

Michael: natal placements	+ precessional increment at 18 arc minutes
☉ ♈ 1 31	☉ ♈ 1 49
☽ ♑ 14 07	☽ ♑ 14 25
☿ ♈ 19 35	☿ ♈ 19 53
♀ ♒ 15 10	♀ ♒ 15 28
♂ ♈ 13 37	♂ ♈ 13 55
♃ ♓ 10 58	♃ ♓ 11 16
♄ ♈ 20 35	♄ ♈ 20 53
♅ ♒ 11 29	♅ ♒ 11 47
♆ ♒ 1 40	♆ ♒ 1 58

♇ ♐ 8 02
☊ ♍ 9 28

♇ ♐ 8 20
☊ ♍ 9 36

Finding Category 1 Transits

From the ephemeris, find the position of the inner planets at midnight on 22 March and again on 23 March. This will show where they are to be found during the twenty-four hours of Michael's birthday.

To these placements, add precession for twenty-one years (50.25 x 21 = 17' 35")

Midnight on March 22nd 2019

☽ ♎ 14 00
☉ ♈ 1 05
☿ ♓ 18 14 ℞
♀ ♒ 24 13

Midnight on March 23rd 2019

☽ ♎ 28 38
☉ ♈ 2 04
☿ ♓ 17 38 ℞
♀ ♒ 25 24

Check each of these placements against:

i) the natal chart (denote r for radix) and
ii) the progressed chart (denote p for progressed).

The Moon: in 8th r & 5th p; ruler of 2nd & 3rd houses r / Asc. & 2nd house p

natal chart

☽□☽ **in 8th r & 5th** p; ruler of 2nd & 3rd r./ Asc & 2nd p.
☽☍♂ **in 11th r& p;** ruler of 6th & 11th
☽△♀ **in 10th r & p;** ruler of 5th & 12th
☽☍☿ **in 11th r & 10th p;** ruler of Asc. & 5th house
☽☍♄ **in 11th r & p;** ruler of 9th & 10th;

progressed chart

☽ ⚻ ♃ **in 10th r & p;** ruler of 6th & 10th p / 7th & 11th r.
☽☍☉ **in 10th p & 11th r;** ruler of 3rd p & 4th r.
☽☍♄ **in 11th r & p;** ruler of 7th, 8th, 9th, 10th p/ 8th, 9th 10th r.
☽☌☽ **in 8th r & 5th p;** ruler of Asc.& 2nd p / 2nd & 3rd houses r.

The Sun in eleventh r and tenth p; ruler of the fourth r and third p

The Sun has returned to its natal placement as one would expect on a birthday, emphasising the sextile between Neptune r and p and in the ninth r and eighth p.

Mercury in eleventh r and tenth p; ruler of asc. and fifth r I fourth and twelfth p.

Mercury is retrograde, but makes no aspect to any planet in the natal or progressed chart.

Venus in the tenth r and p; ruler of the twelfth and fifth r I fifth and eleventh p.

Technically, Venus makes no aspect to any planet on Michael's birthday, but on that day, it is only one degree away from a sextile from Saturn p. This aspect may be considered to be in effect on this birthday.

natal chart	progressed chart
-	♀ ✶ ♄ in 11th r & p; ruler of 7th, 8th , 9th, 10th;

As you will see when we come to interpretation, with Category 1 planets, the houses that the planets rule matter far less than the houses that they occupy in the natal and progressed charts because these indicate the areas of life that feel the impact of the transit activity. But we have given the full workings so that if you have been accustomed to using transits with the planets divorced from their function as significators, this exercise will be good for limbering up. When it comes to Category 3 planets, this kind of information is very important.

Finding Category 2 Transits

Midnight on March 22nd 2019	Midnight on March 23rd 2019
♂ ♉ 23 51	♂ ♉ 24 31
♃ ♐ 23 45	♃ ♐ 23 48

Check both these placements against:

  i)   the natal chart
  ii) the progressed chart.

Mars in the eleventh r and p; ruler of sixth and eleventh r I fifth and eleventh p.

natal chart	progressed chart
-	♂ ☍ ☽ * in 8th r & 5th p; ruler of Asc.& 2nd p / 2nd & 3rd r.

*Advancing orb 2°

Jupiter in the tenth r and p; ruler of seventh and eleventh r I sixth and tenth p.

Remember that precession takes Jupiter into another degree.

natal chart	progressed chart
-	♃ △ ♄ in 11th r & p.; ruler of 7th, 8th , 9th, 10th

Endnotes

1.   Declinational transits

This occurs when, during its orbit, a planet shares the same degree of declination (distance north or south of the equator) as that of another planet. This creates a temporary connection between the two, known as a parallel, and it has the effect of a harmonious minor aspect, which is of significance, especially if no other aspect between two planets is in force.

When one planet is on the same degree of declination, but in the northern hemisphere while the other planet is the southern hemisphere, this is a contraparallel. Its effect is that of a stressful minor aspect, which is also of significance, especially if no other aspect between the two planets is in force.

Orbs of influence are not used here; the planets must be on the same degree of declination.

Declinations are falling out of usage in the astrology software age, but the astrologer prepared to go the extra mile and check for parallels and contraparallels in an ephemeris will be rewarded.

Chapter 2

Category 1 and 2 Transits

Transits by the outer planets, especially to inner planet significators, can produce life-changing experiences. We will look at the outer planets in Chapter 3.

The inner planets, however, play their part because they create the conditions that enable the influences of the outer planets to come through. In terms of human consciousness, this is the same as saying that the inner planets create conditions in the conscious mind that enable the transpersonal planets to find a channel into our personal realities. The inner planets, working through the houses, determine the form through which an outer planet will express itself. They act as a funnel that concentrates and directs the subtler energies of the outer planets.

We have recently lived through a very significant global occurrence. Whatever led up to the events of September 11, it was the configuration made by the inner planets in the charts of the United States that let through the energy that manifested itself as the incidents involving aircraft.

The event-oriented astrologer studies the form very closely. The astrologer whose focus is consciousness will also have a healthy respect for form, because here he will find the point of interface between the transpersonal and the personal. By means of an analysis of the form, he will be able to offer an explanation about the process brought by the outer planet that hopefully will encourage his client to engage with it constructively. These outer planet transits can bring us our best opportunities, and a spiritually aware person needs to know how to think about that and how to use these opportunities progressively.

It is fundamental to esoteric methodology to work from the general to the particular and from the outer to the inner because the lesser contains a scaled-down representation of the greater. It is for this reason that in the first part of this lesson, we described the planets as having different modes: A transit of Pluto to Mars, for example, will bring out Mars' Plutonian mode. At the level of form, the greater contains the smaller, but at the level of being, the lesser contains at least a spark of the greater. This is esoteric understanding, and it connects all things in manifestation.

Transits do not bring to us anything that is not already there. It is important to understand this. They bring out what is in our minds, drawing it to the surface where we confront it in the circumstances of everyday life. It is ourselves whom we are meeting.

In this second part of Chapter 2, we look at the inner planets from this point of view.

Interpreting inner planet transits

All transiting planets are also significators. As they transit, they are representing the house in which they are located and the house or houses that they rule. The planets

they contact are also significators representing areas of life and the things contained within that area of life. The house in which the contact is made is the area of life where this mix of energies will manifest. When working with a transiting planet, always ask yourself: Where does this planet come from and which house(s) does it rule?

Planets Involved in Category 1 Transits

The Moon: Our ever-changing moods

The transiting Moon influences the way we feel about ourselves and our lives at any time. These impressions are not to be confused with our considered assessments. The Moon creates emotional reactions that colour our realities without changing their substance.

The Moon is the fastest-moving planet and is only ever influenced. As it shoots around the chart, it picks up the influences of the planets and weaves the colourful fabric of our moods.

Harmonious contacts may be considered to promote a positive sense; stressful ones promote more challenging perceptions and situations (although in the case of Venus and Jupiter, a stressful aspect may well produce a more constructive and less self-indulgent mood).

The Moon covers one degree of arc every two hours. This means that it is never aligned with any planet for more than a couple of hours, but depending upon the strength of that planet, it can be receiving its influence for some while longer. For example, in the case of Pluto, which has an orb of five degrees approaching and two degrees retreating, this extends the period of Moon-Pluto contact to fourteen hours, during which time the Moon can be making aspects to other planets and blending in this influence.

The influence of the Moon can be a trigger in complex situations, themselves the product of outer planet activity. Often, it will tip the balance between taking action or letting things ride for some while longer, and it is for this reason that tradition recommends waiting three days before acting upon a major decision in order to ensure that it was not the product of a mood.

Using their own charts and the information given in the first part of this chapter, students are encouraged to calculate how long the Moon is held by each of the planets, and using only major aspects, other planets are involved when the Moon makes contact with any natal planet. If, for example, Pluto is in square aspect to Venus natally, Pluto will be activated every time the Moon makes contact with Venus. This will give a very different expression from a transit of Moon to Venus sextile Sun, for example.

The Moon has ten principal modes:

- Solar
- Mercurial
- Venusian
- Martian
- Jupiterian
- Saturnian
- Chironic
- Uranian
- Neptunian
- Plutonian

The Sun: Conferring significance

The Sun, the symbol of the Ego on the mental plane, takes its light wherever it goes. When it contacts an inner planet, it elicits that planet's solar response and makes a person very aware of himself with reference to this energy.

Modern astrology has dropped the term "combust," which was the term given to any inner planet in conjunction aspect with the Sun. When it involved Mercury or Venus, the combust relationship was deemed to be unfavourable by the astrologers pre Second World War (see Endnote 1), especially in its static form in a natal chart, because of the degree of subjectivity involved in the expression of the energy of the combusted planet. It is interesting that modern perspectives do not view this as a negative situation.

At the new Moon, the relationship between the Moon and the Sun, of course, is one of combust, but this term is never used. In Western astrology, if not Hindu astrology, the relationship is viewed favourably rather than not because the Sun regulates the effect of the Moon and our emotional reactions and helps us to see more clearly.

When the contact is harmonious, then a person usually feels positive about himself regarding the planetary principle; when it is stressful, he feels challenged.

The Sun itself has seven principal modes:

- Martian
- Jupiterian
- Saturnian
- Chironic

- Uranian
- Neptunian
- Plutonian

Solar Returns

Solar Returns, which are in charts drawn up in real time for the time that the Sun transits its natal placement, surely owe their popularity to the fact that they are easy to generate. But the level of practical detail that they provide about what is going on and when during the course of a year is inferior to that disclosed by secondary progressions.

They have their place, however. The assumption underpinning a Solar Return chart is that we are reborn every year, and there is something inspirational about that. When used in conjunction with a mental resolve to make a new beginning, the Solar Return gains in value, revealing the themes for the year.

Mercury: Communicating with ourselves and with others

In esoteric astrology, Mercury has a status and significance unknown to orthodox astrology. It is both a sacred planet and the planet that represents the human soul on its own plane. The houses that Mercury rules in the natal and progressed chart are the areas of life through which the soul will communicate to the personality in the circumstances of everyday life.

The pre-war astrologers who identified Mercury combust as an unfavourable situation were wiser than we give them credit for. When the light of the Sun absorbs that of Mercury, a person does not tend to listen to other people, nor does he listen to the voice of his own soul. He hears only the voice of his own personality and becomes isolated.

When transiting Mercury moves into orbs with the Sun in conjunction aspect, we become very locked into our own realities and caught up in detail. It is never a good day for discussions with others. Mercury in stressful aspect with other planets also adversely affects understanding and communication, whilst the harmonious aspects assist.

Mercury has nine principal modes:

- Solar
- Venusian
- Martian
- Jupiterian
- Saturnian
- Chironic
- Uranian
- Neptunian
- Plutonian

Venus: In the light of what we love and what we value

Venus is the planet that represents the love principle, but it also represents our experience of relationship with the people and things in our lives, including the attributes of our own personalities. Esoterically, Venus rules the mental plane where we create our perceptions.

"Bad hair days" occur when transiting Venus is in stressful aspect to a superior planet, and we are likely to dislike aspects of our lives, ourselves, and the way that people relate to us. Our relationships, whether to people, pets, or inanimate objects, seem blighted. If the stressful aspect is with an outer planet, this can produce negative experiences. When Venus is involved in harmonious aspects, our perceptions are more positive.

Venus has eight principal modes:

- Solar
- Martian
- Jupiterian
- Saturnian
- Chironic
- Uranian
- Neptunian
- Plutonian

Inner planet transits are occurring all the time. Students should work with their own charts and an ephemeris to bring consciousness to the experience of these transits and to get a feel for timing.

Planets Involved in Category 2 Transits

Mars: Moving things on

Mars can spring surprises even on astrologers, because it acts in advance of itself and because it acts as a prophylactic. Understanding the role of Mars in releasing energy is crucial in ascertaining the timing of eclipse activity in the planetary sphere, but also in our individual lives.

Transiting Mars, the symbol of the emotional body and, esoterically, the ruler of the astral plane emotionalises wherever it goes, creating anger, enthusiasm, passion, or enervation depending upon the planets that it meets and the aspects that it makes.

Anywhere in the planetary spectrum, Mars moves things on. At the one end, with the Moon, it can create the moods that create waves; at the other, with Pluto, it can produce anger that leads to experiences that can change lives, so profound is its effect, especially when the conjunction and opposition are involved.

Mars has six principal modes:

- Jupiterian
- Saturnian
- Chironic
- Uranian
- Neptunian
- Plutonian

Jupiter: Greasing the wheels of life

Jupiter represents the principle of abundance. When it transits, it brings change through adding more, whether that is more material resource or more confidence. Jupiter is the great unsticker because, for awhile at least, it can make things seem easier, especially when the aspect is harmonious.

Yet with Venus, it can create a perception of facility that can lead to sloppiness, negligence, and indulgence. With Saturn, which is not moderated by Jupiter, as is often assumed, Saturn will take over Jupiter, the faster-moving planet, and uses its expansive quality to enlarge fear. Transits of Jupiter to Saturn (Jupiter in Saturnian mode) especially the conjunction and opposition aspect can send anxiety into overdrive.

Wherever it goes, Jupiter will bring more. Learning to organise ourselves to use this abundance wisely is a life-management skill.

Jupiter has five principal modes:

- Saturnian
- Chironic
- Uranian
- Neptunian
- Plutonian

Example

Using the planet Mars, we will give an example of a transit from a faster-moving planet. This method may be applied to any transit situation.

Mars: Moving things on

Remember that this planet works in advance of itself, and a transit involving Mars is at its most powerful one degree from exact.

The house that Mars occupies and the houses that it rules will be the areas of life about which we can be easily roused to passion. The house and houses ruled by the transited planet will provide an additional but temporary channel for the passions.

With the Moon
Mars dominates the Moon and creates emotional volatility:

- In the case of the harmonious aspects, this can manifest a mood of enthusiasm.
- In the case of the conjunction and the stressful aspects, this can produce irritability and anger.

With the Sun
Mars cooperates with the Sun and creates drive, determination, and energy:

- In the case of the harmonious aspects and the conjunction, this can produce a short period of high energy and activity that gets things done.
- In the case of the stressful aspects, it can manifest frustrating circumstances that thwart the intentions and give us a sense of being incompetent and badly organised.

With Mercury
Mars dominates Mercury and makes that planet express itself in an emotive way:

- In the case of the harmonious aspects and the conjunction, this can produce persuasiveness and emphasis.
- In the case of the stressful aspects, this can produce irritability and angry exchanges.

With Venus
Mars dominates Venus and makes us more assertive in our dealings with others:

- In the case of the harmonious aspects, it enables us to feel confident and take more of an initiative and be more directed and direct with others.
- In the case of the conjunction and the stressful aspects, this can produce a perception of injustice and angry, demanding behaviour that may cause friction and upsets.

With Mars
When transiting Mars meets Mars in the natal and progressed chart, it amplifies the Martian theme. This transit may be felt two degrees both in advance and after the contact is exact:

- In the case of the harmonious aspects and the conjunction, this increases energy arid drive in the areas of life of which Mars is the representative and is a good time for new beginnings.
- In the case of the stressful aspects, it throws up obstacles and difficulties that throw us off course, testing patience and commitment.

With Jupiter

Jupiter dominates Mars and elicits from this planet its Jovian mode, which is enlarging and invigorating:

- In the case of the harmonious aspects, this produces positivity and confidence and a sense that the tasks in hand can be done without too much stress and strain.
- In the case of the stressful aspects, we may lose perspective and give a reckless and unbalanced response to a situation that arouses Mars' passion.
- The conjunction is very high-octane energy, and whether this is used to good effect will depend very much upon whether we have a suitable focus for this energy.

With Saturn

Saturn dominates Mars and elicits from this planet its Saturnian mode, which is subdued and constrained:

- In the case of the harmonious aspects, this can confer determination, resolution, and attention to detail.
- In the case of the stressful aspects, this can produce restrictions and constraints (including illness, particularly flulike conditions) that make a person feel impotent and helpless.
- The conjunction can produce either a determined commitment to a certain line of action or a sense of being beset and overwhelmed by difficulties, which will depend very much upon how well we have learned to deal with challenge.

With Chiron

Chiron dominates Mars and elicits from that planet its Chironic mode which is attention arresting, challenging, and often perplexing because Chiron represents the point of interface between the personality and a higher reality:

- In the case of the harmonious aspects, this can manifest a situation, frequently piquant, that brings clarity and a new understanding in connection with Chironic issues.
- In the case of the stressful aspects, this can manifest situations that leave us unsure of how to respond, leaving us feeling vulnerable and confused.
- The conjunction will be experienced as harmonious or stressful, depending upon our ability to see through form, and to recognise and handle a spiritual challenge.

With Uranus

Uranus dominates Mars and elicits the Uranian response that is decisive and liberating:

- In the case of the harmonious aspects, this produces a sense of confidence, courage, and possibility that enables us to break out of ruts and oppressive situations.
- In the case of the stressful aspects, this can produce circumstances that blow up and are beyond our capacity to control but which leave us freer, although this may not be appreciated or welcomed by the personality.

- The conjunction is very high-octane energy that creates the sense that a situation has developed its own momentum, frequently making us act in a rash manner and act out of character way, but the results are almost always experienced as positive because whatever eventuates, it moves life on.

With Neptune

Neptune dominates Mars, cools its drive and fire, and elicits the Neptunian mode, which is visionary:

- In the case of the harmonious aspects, this can create inspiration and a new, less selfish expression for Martian energy.
- In the case of the stressful aspects, this can produce confusion, tiredness, and a sense of futility.
- The conjunction can produce an altered reality for a short time, which, although we may want to take things quietly at the time, may result in some significant developments after the event.

With Pluto

Pluto dominates Mars and gives intensity to this planet's function of emotionalising:

- In the case of the harmonious aspects, this can give a new kind of awareness that increases or renews commitment.
- In the case of the stressful aspects, this can produce great anger and resentment at things and especially people who thwart the desires and intentions.
- The conjunction produces a depth charge that motivates, shocks, or enrages depending upon our ability to recognise and handle our own emotional reactions.

With the Moon's Nodes

Mars gives its influence to these points in a way that activates tendencies.

- In the case of the conjunction to the north node, this will increase drive and determination to take the kind of action that will move the life on in a way that may be considered progressive.
- In the case of the south node, we may experience distractions in the form of other people or temptations that pull us into old behaviour patterns that we does not like in ourselves or that waste time.

After episodes of significance in their own lives, it is good discipline for students to check out the inner planet transits that were in force at the time of their occurrence.

Endnotes

1. In 1930, Pluto was discovered in far reaches of our solar system. This discovery changed human consciousness, and after the Second World War, astrology developed a different focus and feel, becoming more focused upon the psyche and less concerned with events.

Chapter 3

Category Three Transits:
Saturn and the Outer Planets

When one has worked with transits, it is hard to imagine how astrologers functioned in the days, not really so far back, before the concept of transits entered the body of knowledge used by Western astrology in any meaningful way. But function they certainly did, and it may be of value to consider the explanations that the astrologers of that era gave to the ups and downs of life that we now attribute to transit activity.

For the pretransit astrologers, the fluctuations were part of the turning of the wheel of fortune. Although, presumably, the better times were welcomed and the hard times accepted no less ruefully than we accept them now, there was not the same sense of opportunity within these fluctuations. They were not analysed in the way we analyse them through transit activity, determined to make sense of things and to squeeze something of value out of an experience.

We must also consider that, individually, people were not so sensitive to the workings of the outer planets and experienced them via the collective mind, through the mores and values of their culture, rather than individually. In this respect, World War II is an important watershed. Pluto entered Leo in August 1938, and a new generation began to come into incarnation. This generation was to come to adulthood in the 1960s when the concept of individuality came to dominate thinking.

Prickly and resentful, angry at being held back, but more than a little afraid of breaking free from convention, preoccupied with possibility and fulfilment, creative expression, and sexual emancipation, this generation was the first to directly and consciously experience the effects of the outer planets. The inner and superior planets began to give an enlarged range of expressions as, within the consciousness of individuals, Uranus, Neptune, and Pluto were able to evoke a response from them.

In popular music, for example, the theme of love, hitherto given treatment in one of four modes: having or not having and celebrating or not celebrating, from the 1960s onward became far more varied. As the outer planets began evoking a different consciousness response from Venus and Mars, people had different and more varied experiences of loving, which found their way into expression through popular music.

Remember that transits do not put anything in. They simply bring out what is there, a process which can be undergone more or less consciously.

Astrology has ever reflected man back to himself. And awareness of outer planet transits began to give definition and emphasis to his experience of them. His ability to use them as footholds in time, as he makes his slow and individual ascent through the planes of consciousness was enhanced.

Without doubt, this is the age of the outer planet transit. For spiritually aware people, they are an essential part of working alone and used with awareness they constitute an ongoing exercise in coming to consciousness.

Category 3 transits

The outer planets progress around the zodiac by motions that can be likened to taking two steps forward and one step backward. Saturn's progress, however, is somewhat more direct, and it does not always retrograde over a given point.

With Category 3 transits, it is important to be familiar with each of the three stages created by the transiting planet moving toward and then moving over a planet or hyleg and making a station (stage one); retrograding back over a planet or hyleg and making a station (stage two); and moving forward and clearing the planet or hyleg (stage three).

With Category 3 transits, each of these stages brings with it its own kind of experience.

By contrast, Mercury, Venus, Mars, and Jupiter all go retrograde, but the effect of retrogradation and the difference between their stages is not so marked.

Stage one: Awareness of changing in attitudes in connection with matters signified by the transited planet or hyleg point. This is usually in evidence from five degrees before exact.

Stage two: Between two orders, unable to see a way forward but no longer able to recommit to the old outlook. This is commonly a time of crisis.

Stage three: Change is brought through from the inner to the outer plane and circumstances begin to reflect the new outlook.

Each of these stages is present, regardless of whether the transit is harmonious or stressful.

- If the transit is harmonious, then stages one and three are usually exhilarating, and stage two tends to be a test of patience.

- If the transit is stressful, then all three stages can be challenging in the extreme, but once it is completed, the changes will be absorbed into consciousness.
- When the outer planets go retrograde (stage two), it is a time for contemplation and not action. There is no merit in trying to force issues. This is not always easy to see and accept, if a situation is acutely uncomfortable.

Although different in their ways and means, the effect of all Category 3 transits is to change a person's established way of thinking.

Transiting Saturn

Provoking a decision

ħ

Although conventional astrology puts Saturn with Jupiter in the superior planets category, for the astrologer concerned with the development of consciousness, Saturn, by virtue of the quality of the opportunity that it creates as it transits, needs to be placed with the outer planets.

- Saturn fields the Third Ray within our solar system, and the Third Ray is described in Theosophical tradition as active intelligence or understanding through experience. This is the Ray of Evolution.
- The soul of planet Earth is on the Third Ray, and our planet is said esoterically to express the principle of strength through struggle.
- Saturn rules the throat centre.
- Saturn governs the mental body of the human personality.

When Saturn transits, it elicits the Saturnian response from the transited planet. In this way, Saturn exposes features of the personal reality by manifesting a situation in the outer world. The house that Saturn occupies natally and from which it can be said to come is the major assemblage place of the personal reality. The house that it rules (the areas of life of which is it the significator) are the fields of expression for this reality in everyday life.

Saturn's natural ally is the Moon, which governs form life, but it can be encouraged to serve the Sun.

- In stressful aspect, transits of Saturn expose the rigidity and limitations of our way of understanding in connection with the energy principle represented by the transited planet and are redolent of its lunar affiliation.
- In harmonious aspect, transits of Saturn indicate the potential in our way of understanding in connection with the energy principle represented by the transited planet and testify to its solar connection.

Separate of the Category 3 planets, Saturn's orbit is of a speed that, during a life of average length, brings two Saturn returns (Saturn returning to its natal placement, which occurs for the first time between the ages of twenty-seven and twenty-nine) and increasing numbers of people are experiencing three.

This means that each of the other planets will receive a similar number of transits from Saturn. Each planet could experience the following:

- three transits in conjunction aspect
- six transits in square aspect
- six sextiles
- three oppositions

And, of course, those who live beyond their eighties could experience several more.

In addition to the natal placements of the planets, there are the progressed placements to receive aspects from transiting Saturn.

Separate from all the Category 3 planets, Saturn offers the benefits of accumulated awareness. Will the second transit of Saturn in conjunction aspect to Venus have to manifest the same kind of situations, or will there have been enough change as a result of the first transit for it to take challenge onto a higher level?

From here on into the twenty-first century, Western spiritual ideas can be expected to emphasise personal responsibility and increase awareness of the fact that the quality of our lives is determined by the quality of our decisions. Our conscious decisions can either set us free or lock us into the past.

It is recommended that students to create a chart listing the dates on which Saturn transited a certain planets in the natal chart (the Moon or Venus is a good choice) and make a note from memory of the events and outcomes that coincided with these transits in their own life. Is there a trend in evidence, as well as a theme? Then, look ahead and note the major contacts coming up.

Transiting Saturn provokes situations that require us to make decisions when it transits:

- the Moon
- the Sun
- Mercury
- Venus
- Mars
- Jupiter
- When it transits in stressful aspect, it will evoke the old response that is imbued with memory. This is the line of nil resistance.
- When it transits in harmonious aspect, it will indicate possibilities to be achieved by a progressive decision.

When Saturn transits, it brings clarity of a "warts 'n all kind", eliminating wishful thinking and fantasy from our outlook regarding any particular situation. Saturn exposes the truth of a situation within the reality of any individual. In other words, it shows us the relative truth that is the truth of the personality.

We have several options:

- We can make no decision at all, and let the situation work itself out. Illness or breakdown is frequently a way of avoiding making a decision.
- We can make a decision that would reinforce that within the personality that responds to memory (indicated by the Moon complex; see Endnote 1).

- We can make a progressive decision that eases us just a little closer to fulfilling the goal of the personality (indicated by the personality purpose triad; see Endnote 2).
- We can make a progressive decision from a place of understanding the requirements of the soul-aligned personality (indicated by the soul purpose and personality purpose triad; see Endnote 3).
- We can make a decision that intentionally ignores the relative truth of the personality and attempts to expresses the truth of the soul. This is very difficult for someone working alone, and its effects may not be too dissimilar to those connected with taking the first option. This is because both in their different ways have the effect of circumventing the relative truth of the personality (see Endnote 4).

It is unlikely that a person with no concept of development or any understanding of the principle of strength through struggle would make a progressive decision. He is far more likely to repeat an old and familiar way of being.

Progressive decisions are made consciously not by chance. They require clarity, understanding, and effort. Saturn will provide all those qualities if invited.

Transiting Chiron
Inviting in a higher level

☿

- Chiron fields the Fourth Ray within our solar system, in which it was discovered in 1970s. It is believed to be a visitor from another system.
- It governs the process of reorienting the personality from self-centredness to soul consciousness.

Chiron works through by manifesting situations that cause us disquiet and cause us to question our assumptions about those situations. Unlike transits of Saturn that encourage us to look at the facts of the matter and bring our expectations into line with the truth of our input into a given situation, Chiron brings about situations that require a fresh perspective, because the way that the personality is looking is not adequate, being too self-centred.

Chiron invites us to consider a more inclusive, less self-centred perspective.

It is the function of the Fourth Ray to create ongoing challenges, and to this extent, it is restless energy. No matter how far one has come, the attainment of new perspective will of itself disclose new opportunities and faults that require our attention.

This dynamic is probably most readily recognised when it is at work through the zodiacal sign Sagittarius, which makes us restless for change and betterment

Transiting Uranus
Supervising spiritual development

⛢

- Uranus fields the Seventh Ray within our solar system, the Ray described in the Theosophical tradition as the Ray of Ceremonial Order.
- Uranus rules the Brow centre.
- Uranus governs the Egoic or causal body, the Second Aspect of the soul.

Uranus understands form and values it without being controlled by it. To this extent, it expresses the requirement, described in the Sufi tradition, "to stand in this world and bow in the next."

It supervises the experience in incarnation by deciding the junctures at which form has outlived its purpose and at which the consciousness within that form should be released.

Uranus is not the enemy of form or of personality consciousness, but of crystallisation and self-limitation. Uranus supervises the building of the Egoic body on the mental plane, itself a form, but a form higher than that of the mental body.

The house Uranus occupies in a natal chart indicates the area of life in which a person needs to be freed from the kind of forms around which the personality will consolidate (because it has done so in past life). In this area, it acts as the ambassador of soul consciousness, and the house or houses that it rules, indicate the areas of life that will provide fields of expression for this energy in everyday life, and it may be an exceptional expression.

When Uranus transits, it elicits the Uranian response from the planets that it contacts, encouraging them to free themselves from the forms through which they have been expressing themselves and to find higher forms.

It is the function of the Seventh Ray to find and use those forms and is the basis of magic.

- When the contact is in stressful aspect, then it is challenging to the existing structure of the personal reality and being forced to relinquish that structure can be traumatic to the personality.
- When the contact is in harmonious aspect, then the personal reality is ready to expand and to acknowledge the need to let go of things that have served their purpose, from people to ideas.
- In both cases, Uranus acts through sudden occurrences and unforeseen events. In both cases, it is almost always the case that we can soon understand why that development had to occur, unwelcome or even traumatic though it may have been at the time. Uranus can cut very deep, but those cuts quickly heal.

It takes Uranus eighty-four years to orbit the Sun, and there are now increasing numbers of people experiencing the Uranus Return, which means that they will also have experienced two squares, two sextiles, three trines, and an opposition from Uranus to all other planets and hylegs. When it makes these contacts, Uranus brings out the divine, even though this may announce its presence in the personality as acute restlessness, lawlessness, and erratic behaviour.

The astrologer seeks out major aspects from Uranus because even though he will not be able tell his client what will happen in detail, he knows that this very contact will create an opportunity in connection with the things of which the transited planet is the significator. As would be the case if a hole were made in the wall of a closed room, through this opening will come in new air to freshen the life as a whole.

There will be many such contacts over the course a lifetime. A person who lives to be eighty-four will have known seventy.

The cycle itself is designed to garner the consciousness from form, squeezing the most progressive response out of each opportunity, so that at its close, the tired man can say "It is finished."

Uranus is spiritually ambitious for us.

Transiting Neptune
Admitting a higher reality

$$\Psi$$

- Neptune fields the Sixth Ray of Devotion within our solar system.
- Neptune rules the Crown centre.
- Neptune governs the impulse that moves personality consciousness out of separation and isolation.

Compared to the ways Uranus and Pluto work, Neptune's subtly can cause the personality to underestimate its power and effectiveness. Neptune is not confrontational; rather, it acts through eroding and dissolving the personal reality to find a way in. To this extent, Neptune is subversive of the personality's structures, and it can create muddle and distress. For this reason, orthodox astrologers of the previous century considered it a malefic planet.

The house Neptune occupies in the natal chart indicates the areas of life in which the personality is at its least self-centred and most attuned to the perspectives of the soul. The house (or houses) ruled by Neptune indicates the way that his energy is fielded into everyday life.

- When transiting in stressful aspect, Neptune creates perceptions that pose a serious challenge to the existing structure of the personal reality. Whether those perceptions can be said to be accurate is not the point; the point is that these perceptions will catch us up and alter our way of looking at life. Even if these changed perceptions last for only the duration of a transit, they release us from the grip of a habitual mindset. Even though later we may recoil in disbelief at what they were considering doing (because ideas fostered under stressful Neptunian developments may never come to pass at the physical level), there will have been an exchange between the soul and the personality, the value of which may be beyond the personality to assess.
- When transiting in a harmonious aspect, Neptune creates inspiration and vision that lift us above the limitations of everyday perspectives and bring joy into our lives. The harmonious aspect finds its way into manifestation much easier than the stressful, which is reverse of the customary state of affairs, but then this is exactly how Neptune works: It turns the personality on its head, so that it is disorientated, decentralised, and no longer self-seeking. The Neptunian experience is depicted in the Major Arcana of the Tarot as the Hanged Man.

Neptune represents the third aspect of the soul or the soul-on-its-own-plane: The perspectives of Neptune are not those of the self-seeking isolated personality. As it takes approximately 164 years to orbit the Sun, most of us will die before Neptune has completed much more than half of its orbit, and compared to those from Saturn and even Uranus, we will experience relatively few major aspects from Neptune. The precise number will depend entirely upon the pattern of the planets in the natal chart.

But like those of Uranus, these contacts that evoke the Neptunian response bring out the divine and enable the transited planet to give a response that is soul—and not personality-oriented. They may give us some of the highest moments of our lives, and the fact that they are not sustainable (and they are not) does not make them any less valid. They are what they are, and as experiences, they last as long as they last, but their effects on consciousness last for all time. Personality consciousness cannot comprehend the nature of Neptune, but nor does Neptune require this. Like Uranus and Pluto, Neptune does not require the cooperation of the personality in order to do its work

Neptune's transits bring the transfiguration experience, after which we must be prepared to come down from the mountain, back to the planes of everyday life, subtly changed by what we have seen, more compassionate, better connected to others, and better able to be of service through our lives.

Transiting Pluto
Exposing the roots

- Pluto fields the energy of the First Ray within our solar system.
- Pluto rules the centre at the base of the spine.
- Pluto governs the process of fusing spirit and matter and the biological process of generation.

Of all the outer planets, the workings of transiting Pluto are those that are likely to cause the most perplexity. It is not easy to consciously cooperate with Pluto because it works below the threshold of consciousness. Consciousness can only recognise the need to make room for the process; it cannot hope to control it. With transits of Pluto, understanding of what has been going on often comes after the event.

It is also the case that we are not, in general, comfortable with the idea that in the beginning was darkness within which light grew as a seed. Contemporary spirituality picks up the evolutionary story with the appearance of the light and remains focused on the light and upon the goal rather than the means of transformation. But that darkness is the means of light holds true within the cosmos and within a human being.

Pluto governs that fertile darkness (matter) into which the seed of light (spirit) is sown. If a vegetable is left in the soil in which it has grown, it will simply rot. It is this way with a human consciousness: If we do not move within the fields of experience available to a human being, growth will cease and we will simply vegetate.

In a natal chart, the house in which Pluto is situated indicates the field of experience that has supported the growth of the individual up to this time and of which he is now ready to become more fully conscious in order to create with it the kind of relationship that will permit further growth. The house or houses that Pluto rules indicates the area of life into which consciousness of the need for change and transformation will flow.

As it transits, eliciting the Plutonian response from the planets that it contacts, Pluto exposes that which surrounds the very root of the consciousness associated with that planetary principle. These influences have supported growth, working unseen, below the threshold of consciousness, but there is now a need for a greater awareness of them and to make possible the changes that will permit an individual to move on and enable his consciousness to expand. These influences (social, cultural, religious and racial perceptions) may belong to the collective and not simply the individual.

Pluto governs the decent into matter and the growth of the seed of consciousness. Transits of Pluto disclose attitudes and behaviour, all emotionally based, of which we have been unaware.

This may be uncomfortable and embarrassing to spiritual vanity, but is no less valuable for that. When they have been brought to the surface and exposed to the light, these patterns can be seen for what they are.

- When Pluto transits in stressful aspect, it will ruthlessly disclose what has become an obstruction to further growth, and this will always be negative in relation to the highest expression of the energy of the transited planet of which the personality is capable. For this reason, it may provoke a personal and spiritual crisis.
- When Pluto transits in harmonious aspects, it reveals hitherto unacknowledged strengths and impulses in connection with the energy of the transited planet that encourages us to break into new areas of experience. In this way, we create opportunities that will enable consciousness to expand.

It is a lot to expect a person who is being turned inside out by a transit of Pluto to understand or appreciate the purpose of the process that has caught him up. It is at such times that astrology comes into its own, because a perceptive astrologer may be able to offer an explanation that turns the crisis into a spiritual opportunity.

Transits to the Hyleg Points and Moon's Nodes

As we conclude the section of the transits of the planets, it is important to remind ourselves that unlike the planets the hyleg points, the Moon's nodes are simply points of entry into the etheric field of a human being.

These points cast no rays. They simply admit influence to specific areas of consciousness. The transit therefore is more pure than when a planet, which has its own nature, is involved. For this reason, transits to hyleg points from conjunction and square aspects are very powerful. The impact of sextiles and trims is evident, but not so marked. Indeed, conventional astrology does not acknowledge sextiles and trines to a point that casts no rays, but this is a deduction from a principle rather than an observation. Students are advised to take note of the harmonious aspects.

- Owing to the polar nature of hyleg points and the nodes, a transit to one point will also involve a simultaneous aspect to its opposite point.
- Transits in stressful aspect, particularly those from the outer planets, issue a strong challenge to the existing structure of an individual's reality through situations that may appear to be beyond our control.
- Transits in harmonious aspect encourage an awareness of the need to introduce change into the areas of life signified by the hylegs.
- Where the Moon's nodes are concerned, the important transits are those made in conjunction to either the north (future) or the south (past) node.

Students should ensure that they know which outer planets are at work in their lives at all times and become familiar with the forward / retrograde / forward motions that mean that outer planets transits last many months

Endnotes

1. This is defined and discussed in Part 4 of this author's *Transitional Astrology* (TA/4.) Essentially, it is the Moon and its dispositor, and Saturn and its dispositor.
2. See TA/4: The Sun and the ruler of the Sun sign and the planet disposed by the ruler of the Sun sign.
3. See TA/4: The esoteric ruler of the ascendant and the planet disposed esoterically by the ascendant ruler.
4. An example of this would be turning the other cheek in a situation that was provoking to the personality, because this was believed to be the spiritually correct thing to do at all times, not because the circumstances recommend it. The disregarded personality will react to this on any or all of its three levels. This is a difficult route for people without personal interaction with teachers to help them process the reactions, and it can produce serious dysfunction. Many spiritual aspirants find themselves in this confusing zone.

Chapter 4

Building the Picture

What kind of day Michael can expect on his twenty-first birthday

Prioritising is essential to building a picture:

1. Start with the primary directions.
2. Draw a secondary progressions chart, consider the position of the progressing Moon, and work out secondary directions in force in that month.
3. Consider the Category 2 and 3 planet transits in relation to planets p & r.
4. Consider Category 1 transits in force on the day in relation to planets p & r.

Organising transit information

Before we undertake the exercise in synthesis, we must organise transit information.

recall that we noted the transits in force on Michael's birthday. The purpose of this was to indicate the kind of perspective and the kind of time frame we need to use for studying transits.

For practical purposes, noting those placements on the natal and progressed charts is essential for creating a picture. See the charts in Figures 1 and 2.

Planetary transit category 3	Stage 1	Stage 2	Stage 3
♀□♄r	•		
♀□♄p	•		
♀□☉p	•		
♆♂♃p	•		
♅□♆ r&p	•		
♄□♄r	•		

From these transits, it can be seen that:

- At the time of his twenty-first birthday, Michael, transiting Pluto, will be active. All Pluto's transits will be in stage one, which will mean that although he will be aware of tension in the area of life occupied by Saturn and the Sun (tenth and eleventh houses), at this early stage in the process, he is unlikely to have any real understanding of why his career and friendships are manifesting difficulties. Saturn, as the ruler of Capricorn, is the significator of relationships (seventh p) and emotional attachments (eighth p), so close relationships will be involved in this situation.
- Saturn in stressful aspect is also emphasising this theme.
- The Sun rules the fourth house, indicating tensions in domestic arrangements, with his mother, and in his own emotional balance.
- Neptune's transit of Jupiter (tenth), also in stage one, will be making him aware of different (more visionary and idealistic) ways of thinking about career and lifestyle, but at this early stage, it will be without any clear idea of where this will lead.
- This theme is picked up by Uranus' transit of his ninth house Neptune, which is likely to arouse questioning and spiritual uncertainty.
- Maybe Michael will be undergoing changes of which his friends are more aware than Michael himself. Jupiter is the significator of relationships (seventh r) and work (sixth p). Perhaps Michael will come under the influence of another person around this time who influences his outlook and contributes to these changes of which his friends are aware and are causing tensions between them.

Overall, the picture is of changing attitudes and outlooks that have repercussions on his career and friendships. Even if in the previous year the initial effect of Neptune's contact with natal Jupiter was a sense of elation and adventure, by the time of his birthday, under the influence of Pluto and Saturn, he is likely to be feeling vulnerable, lonely, and insecure.

This, then, is the basic frame of mind at this time.

Category 2
♃ △ ♄ p
♂ ☐ M p

From these transits, it can be seen that:

- Mars and Jupiter, which could bring some energy and passion into this situation, are not able to help out very much.
- Jupiter, in exact trine to Saturn, will be very sober, and as the ruler of seventh and sixth may indicate that a relationship situation (whatever the nature of that relationship) has passed through its honeymoon phase and is becoming more demanding.
- Around the time of his birthday, Mars is advancing fast and provocatively on the MC (remember Mars works in advance of itself) to produce something of showdown in respect of career.

Category 1
♀⚹♄ (separating aspect)
☿℞
☽♎

From these transits, it can be seen that:

- On his birthday itself, transits from the inner planets will not provide much lift. Venus, which natally is the significator of recreational activities (fifth) and by progression is the significator of friends, is still under the influence of Saturn and will be subdued by that contact.
- Although it makes no aspect, Mercury, the ruling planet (and also the significator of recreational activities), is in a retrograde condition that does not benefit outer expression and the Moon is in the sign Libra and in opposition to the planets in Aries.

Bringing it Together

The work done already on Michael's chart at the primary and secondary levels bring over the findings about this period in his life.

i)   Significant primary directions:

age: 19 ☉p♂♄
21 ☿℞⚹♈ᶜ

It is evident from the fact that the progressed Sun makes a conjunction to Saturn at age nineteen that at twenty-one, Michael will be no stranger to difficult circumstances involving friends and career. Owing to the retarding effect of Saturn, the effect of that contact at the primary will be felt into and through his twentieth birthday year.

Meanwhile, transiting Pluto, coming out of sixth and sixth (fifth by progression) will be advancing on natal Saturn, progressing Saturn, and the progressed Sun itself, taking this trying process to a new stage by making him aware of deep-rooted and unconscious attitudes and assumptions toward work, service, and his own physicality. Saturn's square to Saturn will push him to make some decisions in this birthday year.

The fact that at the primary level, Mercury will be in retrograde at this time, however, will increase Michael's capacity to handle the challenge of this process that will be urging him to bring consciousness to bear on the way he is living his life.

Retrograde Mercury may not benefit outer expression, but it is very supportive of self-analysis, review, and inner understanding. The fact that, in this retrograde condition, Mercury makes a sextile to the ascendant indicates that Michael will be able to link his awareness with his way of interacting with others.

ii)   Significant secondary influences

There are no secondary directions in force in March, the time of Michael's birthday. The progressing Moon itself is moving through the fifth house of the progressed chart (fifth and sixth house of the natal chart), making individuality and creative (including sexual) expression the themes around which he will be assembling impressions.

It should be noted that by the time of his twenty-first birthday, the progressing Moon will be moving away from an opposition to the progressed Sun. This will be exact some six months earlier, creating a climax in the ongoing matter of self and others (eleventh/fifth theme). As the Moon moves into the waning phase of the cycle, he can be expected to be trying to make changes in his way of working and living that are expressive of a new awareness.

Conclusion

This is a stressful and difficult time for Michael, which cannot be expected to reach any kind of resolution until Pluto clears Saturn (r and p) and the Sun (p) for the final time. This will not occur until the autumn/winter of 2020, when he is well into his twenty-second birthday year.

Not even his twenty-first birthday offers much levity, falling as it does in the midst of a time of tension in personal relationships.

Given that there will be so much pressure upon him at this time, the most helpful feature is the retrograde condition of his ruling planet, Mercury, which will make him inward-looking, introspective, and willing to cooperate the best he can with the required review.

Michael is unlikely to remember his early twenties as being an easy and carefree time. It is to be hoped that this kind of pressure, coming at a relatively young age, will help him to find his true identity, which is that of a group-oriented, idealistic, forward—looking person.

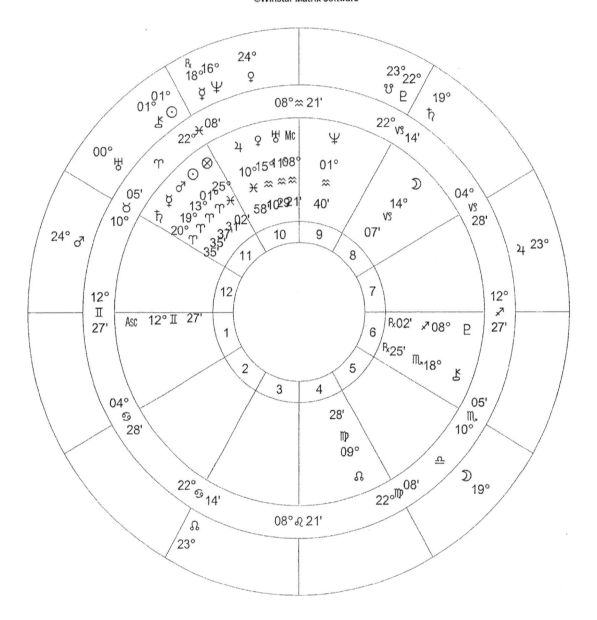

Figure 1 Michael: natal chart with planetary transits on March 22nd 2019
Geocentric, Tropical, Koch house system
©Winstar Matrix software

Figure 2 Michael: progressed chart (21ˢᵗ birthday year) with planetary transits
for March 22ⁿᵈ 2019
Geocentric, Tropical, Koch house system
©Winstar Matrix software

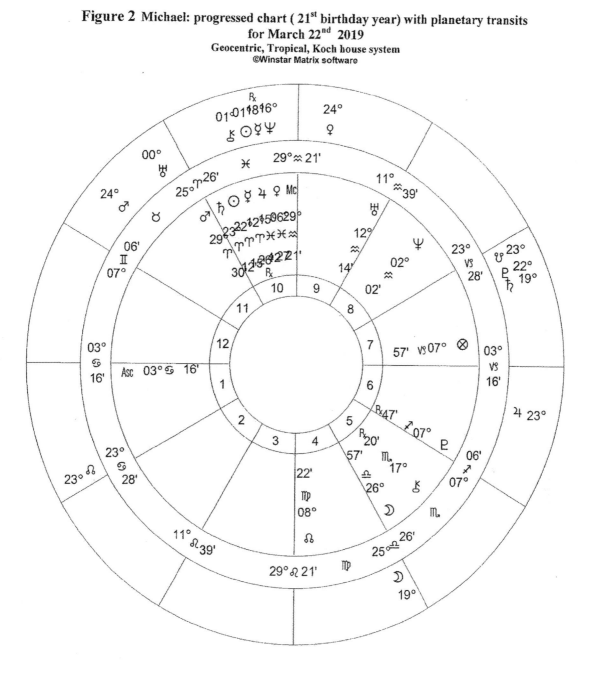

Part Three

Practical Tips on Working with Time

Looking at the Context

Introduction

Nothing stands still; we know that as observers of everyday life.

Esotericists are aware that spiritual truths may be timeless, but the ways they are offered are not. Spiritual truths have to be repackaged constantly to reflect changes brought by time. As astrological practitioners, we must be prepared to review regularly the approach and methods we use to ensure that we are still communicating. We have a responsibility to be sensitive to the sound of what we are offering. There are few things more unhelpful to someone who is truly seeking guidance than a delivery that is out of date and uses terminology that sounds judgemental, threatening, or priggish. That cannot and will not inspire.

In this, the second decade of the twenty-first century, clients are coming for readings with attitudes, expectations, and a relationship to spirituality that are quite different from those in evidence during the first, and which were themselves different from those of the clients of the 1980s and 1990s.

This reflects the fact that new generations, with different existential issues are coming through. The basic questions remain the same, however: What is my purpose? How and where should I steer my life? What is the role and place of relationship in my life?

For as long as these are questions that bring clients to astrologers, the natal chart supplemented by the primary directions, secondary progressions, and the transits in force retain their value as basic documents to prepare in advance of any reading situation. These documents identify an individual's developmental purpose and provide a context in which to place that life.

How to best deliver that information remains the astrologer's question and one we have to answer for ourselves, again and again.

1. Establishing the Anatomy of a Situation

If an astrologer has progressed the natal chart and prepared the primary and secondary directions, as well as noted the transits, he has an anatomy of the present time in front of him and can answer crucial questions in advance of the reading.

Question	Refer to
What are the planetary principles involved in the situation?	Look at primaries in force and at major outer planet transits
Where does it fit into the all-important 28 year & the solar-lunar cycle?	Secondary chart, specifically the house position of the progressing Moon
If it part of any other significant cycle e.g., the cycle of Saturn?	Natal chart and ephemeris
How long is the situation likely to retain its intensity or, if there is a pause in the situation, because a key outer planet is retrograde, when will it become more insistent again?	See Processes (below)
When will opportunities enter this situation in the form of Uranian, and to a lesser extent, Jupiterian activity?	See Processes (below)
When will it be time for decisions?	See Processes (below)
What does the client need to understand about the present situation?	Natal chart – life themes
Are old patterns in evidence in this situation?	Natal chart, specifically the Moon & Saturn
What is going to be a progressive outcome?	Position of the Sun

All these questions are answerable if the astrologer has the primary and secondary directions to supplement the natal chart.

The client's immediate reason for visiting is more than likely to be found in the present situation and without prompting from the client, it may be a good strategy for the astrologer to comment upon the quality of the present time. This will do a lot to reassure the client that the astrologer is on the case.

To see the anatomy of the present time is not the same as knowing all the details, and the client should be encouraged to describe his or her experience of the present. Encouraging a client to talk about the present situation is invaluable in the gauging of how a client is responding to the challenge of his or her own life.

There is rarely a problem about getting detail, but do be aware that testimonies are only ever going to be a part of the whole story. Whatever the tone of the client's presentation, it is up to the astrologer to assess what is being related against the anatomy of the present time. This itself is revealing.

If a client is making light of a stressful transit of Pluto to the Moon, for example, the astrologer needs to ask questions designed to find out whether there is more that the client could tell, pose the relevant questions, and make the kind of observations based on an understanding of how painful such a transit usually is to see if the exchange can be taken onto a deeper level.

Alternatively, the descriptions given by the client may be so graphic and presented with such drama that the astrologer will have a struggle both to get in word in and keep the larger picture in view.

If the client truly wants the astrologer's contribution, the astrologer must be allowed to speak! Reading room disciplines are essential because the time available can be so easily used up by a client who is allowed to forget that he or she has come for a fresh interpretation of events, not to air, yet again, the familiar perception.

In the final analysis, it is the responsibility of the astrologer to ensure that the details that have been given have been fitted into a larger picture and that the client has been offered a new perspective with which to work. It is a new perspective that turns a crisis into an opportunity.

Whatever has occurred and wherever the client is with it, what has unfolded is a part of that person's story. Things go wrong only in perception; the reality is that things work the only way that they can, based upon what has gone before and the new energies entering the situation. The astrologer must assume that any situation, no matter how difficult or traumatic, could lead to something positive and the client should be offered this way of understanding. It could be a lifeline, because the reading room is a place of great receptivity. Dead ends, like problems, exist only in the perception.

2. Processes

The client experiences situations; the astrologer sees processes. Processes are made by consciousness from the raw material of occurrences in time. The astrologer is an agent in this creative situation.

To the astrologer, life is a succession of processes that manifest situations in everyday life. Some of these processes may overlap in time, but at any one time, there will be one process that dominates the others.

- Major transits of outer planets last eighteen months to two years, and when in force, they will be the dominant influence.
- If there is an important primary direction in force, this will set the tone for that birthday year.
- Transits of the superior planets will dominate if neither of the previously mentioned are in force.
- The phase of the twenty-eight-year cycle of the progressing Moon will show where the impressions created by these experiences are being assembled.

Processes have a beginning, a middle, and an end. To put this another way, they comprise:

- the initial challenging phase when a person faces new developments in relation to the matters signified by the planet receiving influences from either a progressed planet or a transiting planet

- the period of review when a person is required to assess the changes brought about by the new developments and to consider his or her response
- the period of conclusion when a person brings into outer expression the changes in awareness brought about by the process. This concluding phase may well bring new situations to which a response is required. This is the time when the most effective decisions can be made

These three phases are most obvious when the process is being brought about by a transit, but it is still evident in a progression:

- The initial phase is brought about by the progressing planet advancing on the significator.
- The period of review occurs when the contact is exact. This corresponds to the state known as occultation in astronomy when one celestial body is hidden by another (usually the Moon).
- The concluding phase comes when the progressing planet moves away from an exact contact.

All processes are designed to move us on in consciousness toward a fuller expression of our true identity, which is described by the position of the Sun in the natal chart.

Processes fall into two broad categories:

- eliminating old ways of thinking and being
- adding new awareness

These two kinds of processes eventually lead to the same place: a change in awareness. The journeys, however, are likely to be very different.

Processes that eliminate old ways of thinking and being

These processes bring the most discomfort and are brought by:

- Stressful aspects at the primary level, especially those involving the two luminaries
- Saturn and the outer planets in aspect to the luminaries and the hylegs.
- Stressful transits of Saturn and the outer planets to both luminaries and the hylegs.
- The movement of the progressing Moon through any of the water houses (fourth, eighth, and twelfth houses).

Stressful aspects at the secondary level (from the Moon to natal and progressed planets) add their weight to whatever processes are in force at that time, but as they last only one month, they cannot themselves be said to constitute a process.

Teacher John de Ruiter has a saying: "The only thing in your mind is what you have put there." And astrologers see that the only things in our lives are what our minds have attracted to us. Our circumstances externalise what is in our minds.

In the initial phase of a process when a person faces the challenges from new developments, these challenges come from the unfolding of the design of his or her own personality, but if the outer planets are agents in the issuing of that challenge, they are coming from beyond personality consciousness and will be perceived as coming from the outside.

If the challenge is issued by a progressing planet advancing on another in the natal chart, it is much easier to appreciate that this is the product of the inner geometry.

Provided it is not said with an air of judgment, clients may benefit from being reminded that what they are going through is unfolding from within themselves and that they will be the beneficiary of this process, provided there is a willingness to see the gains in terms of growth and not in terms of the fulfilment of the desires.

When people hear this for the first time, they usually neither understand it nor believe it, but eventually, we all have to come to understand it if we are to know freedom.

Eliminating processes:

1. Stressful transits involving
   - the planet giving the process its name
   - luminaries (Sun natal and progressed; Moon natal)
   - inner and superior planets (natal and progressed)
   - hyleg points (natal and progressed)

2. Stressful aspects at the primary level between:
   - the luminaries
   - the Sun and inner planets
   - superior planets and the luminaries
   - outer planets and the luminaries and inner planets

3. The movement of the progressing Moon through any of the water houses (fourth, eighth, and twelfth houses).

Eliminating process	Defined by stressful aspect of:	Nature	Features
Plutonian	• Transiting Pluto to the luminaries, inner planets & hylegs (natal & progressed). • Progressing Sun, inner planets & superior planets to Pluto (natal & progressed).	Scours the desire nature and brings unconscious patterns to light.	Obsessions; emotional turmoil and loss.
Neptunian	• Transitting Neptune to the luminaries, inner planets & hylegs (natal & progressed). • Progressing Sun, inner planets to Neptune (natal & progressed).	Dissolves rigid mental structures and creates greater sensitivity of others and awareness of a higher reality.	Confusion; delusion; erosion of energy and short term memory.
Uranian	• Transiting Uranus to the luminaries, inner planets & hylegs (natal & progressed). • Progressing Sun, inner planets & hylegs (natal & progressed) to Uranus (natal &	Eliminates attachments on all levels that have served their purpose; liberation.	Unforeseen and shocking situations that have dramatic impact but clear quickly; losses; rebellion and repudiation; severances.

	progressed).		
Chironic	• Transiting Chiron to the luminaries, inner planets & hylegs (natal & progressed) • Progressing Sun, inner planets & hylegs to Chiron (natal & progressed).	Reactivates old (including past life) issues that have been a cause of spiritual confusion and distress.	Situations involving existential or moral issues or personalities with spiritual authority with which the personality does not feel qualified or knowledgeable enough to deal.
Saturnian	• Transitting Saturn to the luminaries, inner planets & hylegs (natal & progressed). • Progressing Sun, inner planets and hylegs to Saturn (natal & progressed).	Externalizes mental patterns that are restricting development and creating imbalances.	Situations involving constraint and requiring much effort and application; the need for conscious decisions is essential if there is to be change.
Primary	Progressing Sun & planets to natal luminaries and planets.	Sets the theme for a birthday year; the backdrop for transits and secondary activity.	Situations of conflict in connection with the planetary principles involved and areas of life of which they are the significators.
Secondary	• Progressing Moon through the Water houses.	Brings a period of 2 - 5 years in which the circumstances of life require a person to look inwards and review and reassess their way of conducting themselves and their lives. It is frequently a lonely and introspective time.	The focus of consciousness becomes: • In the fourth house: the personal past; the home and relationship with the family, especially the mother. • In the eighth house: close personal relationships, and

			the way of interacting, seeking involvement with and recognition from others. • In the twelfth house: the way that the life and time have been used (in the previous 28 years); the consequences of decisions made in that time; the point of the life.

Processes that bring opportunity

Patterns can be changed in one of three ways:

- eliminating some of the features
- adding to the existing features
- reorganising the constituents

The human psyche is made up of patterns, and the processes that we experience in time are designed to bring about changes in those patterns

In the previous section, we looked at the processes that change pattern through elimination and through separating us from the things that we assume, consciously or unconsciously, that we need to ensure our continuity. To some degree, these processes that involve elimination also bring about a certain amount of reorganisation of the existing features. The other side of a major Plutonian process, for example, a person has a changed understanding of self and life, even though the process itself may have focused upon particular issue and a particular area of his or her life.

In this section, we look at the processes that change patterns by supplementing the existing with the new.

To take an opportunity takes more than being given opportunities; it involves recognising an opportunity. We are surrounded by opportunities that our habitual way of looking at life does not enable us to see them as having applicability for us.

During the processes that change patterns through adding new awareness, the way of looking at life becomes more fluid and positive, and this creates the preconditions for the recognition of opportunity.

It is questionable whether it is technically correct to say that the harmonious aspects bring anything into manifestation; rather, they create a receptivity that is able to pick up on what is already there, although that is probably a quibble. Nevertheless, it will be noted that during periods of major new activity, there will be some stressful aspects in force, particularly from transiting planets, or Saturn will be active in harmonious aspects (see Endnote 1).

Initially, opportunities require us to take on something additional. Later, we may have to let go of certain things to make room for the new opportunity, but this is not part of opportunity per se. Like the eliminating processes, the processes that add are also to some degree processes that involve reorganisation.

Identifying periods of opportunity is a very valuable service for the astrologer to provide, but he or she will not be able to offer this if there is no familiarity with time-working techniques. Often, a period of opportunity will come toward the close of an eliminating process and may help to bring a trying and critical time to a close. Identifying the positive in this time-specific way can help a person accept that the eliminating process, painful though it may be, is purposeful.

To encourage a person to make space for a coming period of opportunity is also a helpful service to provide. We live in pressured times and do not always know how to think positively about easing up and relaxing routine to let in new opportunities.

An astrologer may also have to help a client recognise the kind of situations that represent opportunities for him or her specifically and to explain why that should be.

Supplementing processes

1. Harmonious transits involving
   - the planet giving the process its name
   - luminaries (Sun natal and progressed; Moon natal)
   - inner and superior planets (natal and progressed)
   - hyleg points (natal and progressed)

2. Major harmonious aspects at the primary level between:
   - the two luminaries
   - the Sun and inner planets
   - superior planets and the luminaries
   - outer planets and the luminaries and inner planets

3. The movement of the progressing Moon through the fire houses (first, fifth, and ninth).

Harmonious aspects at the secondary level (from the Moon to natal and progressed planets) add their weight to whatever processes are in force at that time, but as they last only one month, they cannot themselves be said to constitute processes.

The periods marked out by the progressing Moon's movement through the fire houses are periods of experimentation, expansion, and new initiatives. This creates a very suitable mental climate for breaking new ground and recognising opportunity.

Supplementing process	Defined by harmonious aspect of:	Nature	Features
Plutonian	• Transiting Pluto to the luminaries, inner planets & hylegs (natal & progressed). • Progressing Sun, inner planets & superior planets to Pluto (natal & progressed).	Gets the positive out of the desire nature by challenging a person to conquer fears, recognise aspirations and draw on inner strengths to give a new and more creative approach to familiar situations.	The return of familiar conditions, sometimes the return of personalities with whom there is unfinished business.
Neptunian	• Transiting Neptune to the luminaries, inner planets & hylegs (natal & progressed). • Progressing Sun, inner planets to Neptune (natal & progressed).	Creates understanding and inspiration which dissolve limitations and sees new possibilities; expands rigid mental structures and creates greater sensitivity of others and awareness of a higher reality.	Situations, interests and people who are inspirational; idealism and aspiration become a motivating force in everyday life.
Uranian	• Transiting Uranus to the luminaries, inner planets & hylegs (natal & progressed). • Progressing Sun, inner planets & hylegs (natal & progressed) to Uranus (natal & progressed).	Enables a person to move on from a situation which in the past has been a source of restriction.	Sudden changes of heart brought about by experiences that may have no direct connection to the issues in which a person is caught; strokes of luck and sudden invitations which require an immediate response.
Chironic	• Transiting Chiron to the luminaries, inner planets & hylegs (natal & progressed). • Progressing Sun,	Heals and diminishes spiritual dilemmas and obstacles.	Encounters with people who represent a higher level of being; situations that enable a person to

	inner planets & hylegs to Chiron (natal & progressed).		come by a different way of understanding in a matter that had caused spiritual unquiet or confusion.
Saturnian (see Endnote 2)	• Transiting Saturn to the luminaries, inner planets & hylegs (natal & progressed). • Progressing Sun, inner planets & hylegs to Saturn 9 natal & progressed).	Creates the opportunities of the future by preparing the ground.	Situations that require effort and application but the purpose and benefits of this are usually obvious and this has implications for the decisions that will be required.
Jupiterian	• Transiting Jupiter to the luminaries, inner planets & hylegs (natal & progressed). • Progressing Sun, inner planets and hylegs to Jupiter (natal & progressed).	Creates mental flexibility and adventurousness.	Material abundance; the lifting of restrictions; new encounters.
Primary	• Progressing Sun & planets to natal luminaries and planets.	Sets the theme for a birthday year; the backdrop for transits and secondary activity.	Situations of co-operation in connection with the planetary principles involved and areas of life of which they are the significators.
Secondary	• Progressing Moon through the Fire houses. .	Brings a period of 2 - 5 years in which the circumstances of life require a person to breathe out and embrace the new. It is frequently an active and adventurous time.	The focus of consciousness becomes: • In the first house: reorganising the lifestyle to admit more of what is considered important and that will add quality and authenticity. • In the fifth house: the creativity and the extent to

			which a person is able to gain respect and recognition from others. • In the ninth house: the spirituality and sense of being a part of something higher and more significant than self at that time; the point of the life.

3.   Decision making

It is only when the process is far enough advanced for a new perspective to be available will progressive decisions be made. The concluding phase is the time for making significant decisions in relation to the issues that are central to the process.

A significant decision is to be understood as one that makes a difference to the unfolding of the situation and changes the individual's position within it.

It is commonly the case that we to try to make significant decisions before decisions are ready to be made. Usually, we experience some reason why we cannot do this.

- Often, this is because we have no control over events. We may never gain control over events (for example, the unwelcome break up of a relationship that results from a partner's loss of commitment), but in time, as a result of the new awareness brought by the process and inner resolve, they may be able to steer our reactions to these events in a progressive way.
- Or if we do make a decision, we soon realise that it has not properly addressed the issue and we have to return to it. This can undermine confidence.
- Sometimes, it will be because we are resistant to acknowledging the need to make a decision at all. Generally speaking, however, the perceived need to make a decision and to take action is a huge cause of stress in the lives of the people we are today, as we respond to the growing awareness that we are responsible for our own lives.

Enhanced awareness permits a greater intuitive awareness of timing, but averagely developed people are now pressured and controlled by time.

The second phase of a process (which is when the transiting planet is in retrograde or the progressing planet is occulting) is the time when we will experience maximum confusion, distress, and a sense of impotence. An astrologer who understands timing can do much to ease this pressure and reassure.

Our decisions are the key that releases us from fate, and the timing of the turning of this key is of extreme importance.

Astrologers should encourage clients to hold off making as many decisions as possible until the process itself has advanced sufficiently and has created a new awareness. This is in the concluding phase of the process.

If we are to use time well and make it work for us, we have to make it our ally. Astrology permits us to see the design of the personality and how it interfaces with the soul and also shows how to work with the in breath (contemplation and elimination) and the out breath (action and opportunity) to move forward. The astrologer who would give this kind of guidance must make time working techniques part of his or her repertoire.

Endnotes

1. The trine and the harmonious conjunctions are most important here. The sextile aspect is supportive of the status quo, and although it may bring acceptance and reconciliation that may amount to a changed attitude of itself, it will not bring opportunities that change circumstance.
2. Saturnian processes, even those brought by harmonious aspects, are not experienced as expansive situations, and as such, they stand out from the other supplementing processes. Logically, however, they must be included because the gains of the Saturnian processes are significant and enduring.

About the Author

Suzanne Rough is a philosophy graduate and has been a practicing astrologer and teacher since 1989. Between 1994 and 2006, she was tutored by Master Djwal Khul (D.K.), and in 1998, she established The DK Foundation School of Astrology in order to share his insights and encourage the next generation of astrology practitioners

About the Book

Working with Time deals with the matter of using the time frames, which enable astrologers to identify the opportunities available to us at any given stage in our lives. By supplementing the natal chart with primary directions, secondary progressions, and transits, an astrologer can build a detailed picture of any year of life and see the forms that opportunity will take at this time. This book shows how to work with these time-working techniques and offers a new perspective on difficult times and situations. All times of change are opportunities if we understand their nature and their purpose and know how to engage with them.

Working with Time is recommended to astrology practitioners and to students with a working knowledge of horoscopy.